THE DEAN TAVERN
A GOTHENBURG EXPERIMENT

ALASDAIR
ANDERSON

For the people of Newtongrange

First published 1986 by
The Dean Tavern Trust
Newtongrange

© Copyright 1986 Alasdair Anderson

The Dean Tavern Trust is grateful to Tennents Caledonian Brewery for financial assistance in the production of this book.

Front cover: Free beer night in 1949 to celebrate 50 years of the Dean
Frontispiece: The opening of the Bowling Green, 1902.

Printed by Spectrum Printing Company, Livingston

CONTENTS

CONTENTS

FOREWORD

In writing a foreword for any book, you're always supposed to say what a privilege it is to be asked. Sometimes this is said sincerely, sometimes not. Let there be no doubt, however, about what I feel about this foreword and indeed about the book itself. I am not only privileged, I am honoured. When you think about the thousands of books published each year, you must also wonder how many are *worth* publishing. Certainly the vast majority of them rise briefly, and sink, deservedly, without trace. Alasdair Anderson's account of the Dean Tavern and, concurrently, of life in Newtongrange in the days gone by, is clearly worth a place on any library shelf indefinitely.

It is history in the best and truest sense of the word. Not the traditional rubbish concerning the antics of kings and queens and various assorted dukes—although a few minor aristocrats are inevitably mentioned in context—but a history of real people and places. Although a work of research—and enormous research—it is never boring. For the people of Newtongrange proud of their heritage as a mining community, it is a fascinating and invaluable book. It would have been a great shame had this book not been written. We should be grateful that there was somebody like Alasdair so willing and so able to write it. Of course, there is a very special reason why I should feel personally honoured to be permitted this very minor contribution. For the first 22 years of my life, I lived—no, not in Nitten—but in Gorebridge. Or, to be more precise, in Birkenside, which may reasonably be called a high-class suburb of Gorebridge. In the immediate vicinity of these three jewels—Arniston, Gorebridge and Birkenside—there were three pits, when I was a schoolboy, anyway. Newtongrange had only two, but we needn't elaborate on that. Suffice to say that, like just about everybody else in that corner of Midlothian, I used to be lulled to sleep, nightly, not by a lullaby but by the fairly-melodious sound of clanking wagons.

Strange to remember that Newtongrange and Arniston are separated only by a very short stretch of straight road—less than a mile, I'd think, though I've never measured. From the Lady Vic to Newtonloan Toll. "The Ropes", they called that stretch then, and probably still do. But that's the geographical distinction. In some ways, it could have been many a mile. In the 1930's and the 1940's, which was just about the time I spent in Gorebridge, we very seldom went near Newtongrange, except, naturally, to pass through or to stop off at Victoria Park for a couple of hours. By the same token, Nitten folk seldom ventured up the braes, not even, unfortunately, to soak up the cultural atmosphere. It has been said that they would always be too easily recognised by their pointed heads and shambling gait, knuckles trailing on the ground but, quite frankly, I believe that to be a serious exaggeration. Returning to the occasions when we would visit the uncharted territory that was Nitten, well, we had to admit they didn't have a bad picture-house. The Palace, no less, and it even had a Balcony.

Dundas Hall, while a superior establishment in terms of quality of films shown—they took different distributors and we had both Cagney and Bogart—there was no balcony.

Now, of course, both are closed, anyway, sacrificed to the great god TV.

Then there was Victoria Park, home of Newtongrange Star, a somewhat minor outfit compared with Arniston Rangers, but again, you see, there was a structural difference which we envied a little. The Star had, still has, a grandstand.

And yet again, the quality of our product was superior, but neither old nor new Newbyres Park had a grandstand. As Alasdair points out, however, a game between the Star and Arniston Rangers was always an event of much significance. In terms of rivalry, it matched an Old Firm game but without the nastiness. But, as Alasdair also says, the rivalry was good natured and—despite any lighthearted comments I may have made earlier—was based on mutual respect.

Certainly there was no segregation of spectators. There was a remarkable mutual trust, too. Before the start of a game, a common sight was that of a fan or fans walking round the track waving, say, a ten-bob note and shouting, "Ten bob back the Star". Or, naturally, "Ten bob back Arniston". From the crowd would come: "Gie's half-a-croon O' that, Jimmy", or "Ah,ll hae it, Dougie". The man with the note didn't always know exactly who he was betting with, but that didn't matter. Everybody always paid. It was a matter of honour. Leafing through Alasdair's book almost at random, there are gems on just about every page.

For example: the Newbattle parish minister, the Rev John Thomson, who doubtless thought of himself as a Christian, and his comments—actually written down—on the "lower orders of society". That was in 1839. The good minister was worried about these lower orders having too many facilities for drinking. Nearly 150 years later, we can read that chapter and marvel on changing attitudes. Or can we? Sometimes, I wonder. For example: the choice given to Nitten miners as recently as 1932. You can have bathrooms and back kitchens, gentlemen, OR pithead baths. A little more than a half-a-century ago, and that was what they thought of the "lower orders". But again, one wonders . . . have attitudes really changed all that much? Think of what was happening to mining communities NOT 150 years ago, NOT 50 years ago, but two years ago! On a more cheerful and more refreshing aspect, the book deals, reasonably enough, with the drinking habits of the miners in the early days. The research is exhaustive and illuminating, the reportage expert. What a wealth of history and memory you'll find in Chapter 13, the grandpa who had his own seat in the Dean—not the only one so privileged—the wee jug bar, and the present he'd bring home every Saturday to his granddaughter. For her, a comb or hair grips, maybe.

For me, on a Saturday, it was a twopenny bar of Duncan's Hazelnut from my grandpa who worked at the Emily. There was no better chocolate ever made aywhere.

And throughout, so deservedly, the Dean Tavern, an institution if ever there was one, is at the core of the book. To call the Dean a pub is like calling Dave Mackay a mere footballer. It is unique. Happily, it is likely to remain so. I needn't tell anybody reading this book why it is unique. Everybody will know.

But consider what would happen to the Dean, if ever one of the big brewers got their hands on it. In no time at all, you'd have a low roof, fancy carpets, juke-boxes, imitation-leather booths, trendy lighting, and all the other manifestations of the tarting-up syndrome. But that, I know, would happen only over the bodies of Willie Yuill and the greater part of the male population of Nitten.

One of my regrets, I suppose, is that the Dean is in Nitten and not up the braes, but, well, the Germans can't win all the time. At least, we have Willie's son in charge of the old Brunton's pub, immediately overlooked by the Birkenside house where I was born and brought up.

But let me conclude the way I began. It's an honour to be a tiny part of this book, a genuine and vital contribution to the present time and, above all, to the future. To Alasdair Anderson, thanks—and congratulations.

JOHN FAIRGRIEVE

THE DEAN TAVERN

There can be few, if any, public houses in Scotland to compare with the Dean Tavern. Not only has the Dean retained its original role as benefactor to the village of Newtongrange but over the years it has developed a character and atmosphere which is quite unique.

There may be many opinions as to why this should be but perhaps the most obvious one is that the Dean has resisted the trend of wholesale modernisation and the introduction of so called "improvements" while at the same time maintaining a high standard of service to its customers.

There is, however, one other important feature which sets the Dean apart and that is the minute books which trace its history from the very first meeting in 1899 to the present day. For that we are indebted to those early committee members who insisted on keeping such neat and meticulous records. As I read through these Minute Books it became apparent that they were not simply an account of the Deans activities but an interesting insight into the development and growth of Newtongrange. I also believed that the story contained in these books would be of interest to others both within and beyond Newtongrange and so the idea of the book was conceived. To find someone who could tackle such a job was easy. I have known Alasdair Anderson for several years and of his interest in local history. Alasdair needed little persuasion and so the project was set in motion. That was over two years ago and since then Alasdair has researched, interviewed, sought out old photographs and read through numerous documents until what had simply been a good idea has become a reality. Alasdair has dedicated his book to the people of Newtongrange and for that we must all be grateful for he has spent countless hours in producing it. However, I am quite sure that there will be many others outside Newtongrange who will read and enjoy his book.

Councillor James Green,
Chairman,
Dean Tavern Trust

Introduction

The Dean Tavern and the village of Newtongrange are inextricably connected and I have attempted to record their joint history side by side. It seemed appropriate to include a section on the early history of coal mining in the area, as well as a chapter on previous local drinking establishments. There is even a chapter on the Bottom Shop!

I have often been asked how the Dean got its name and also how Murderdean Road got its name. The two are connected but I cannot claim to have solved the mystery. Murderdean is the name of the burn that runs beside the road. The 'dean' part of it is Anglo Saxon meaning a wooded valley. I had a theory that the 'murder' part of it was a corruption of Muirton, as there was a place near here called Muirtondean in the 17th century, but now I am not so sure. It is certain that the name of the first Lothian Coal Company housing scheme, Deanpark, begun in 1898, was derived from Murderdean. The first three houses in the scheme were set aside for the Coal Company public house and it was named the Dean Tavern after Deanpark.

Until 1900, the name of the village was written as two separate words and I have used the form 'Newton Grange' until that date and 'Newtongrange' thereafter. Of course, 'Nitten' is the local nickname for the village and has been for a long time. An 18th century map calls the place 'Nooton', maybe that is an early form of Nitten.

I have received enormous help and co-operation from the people of Newtongrange in researching this book and I am very grateful to everyone. A full list of acknowledgements appears at the end of the book. I would particularly like to thank Jim Green, Willie Yuill, Joe Gardiner, Jim Barton, Bob Ross and Jim Reid for their help. The meticulous research carried out by Mike Cotterill, when he worked at the Mining Museum has proved invaluable. The maps used are reproduced by permission of the National Library of Scotland. Extracts from the Dalkeith Advertiser are reproduced by permission of the British Library and Scottish County Press, Dalkeith.

Chapter 1

Early Coal Mining in Newbattle

The earliest records of coal mining in Scotland are contained in a charter granted to Newbattle Abbey in 1210 for lands held by the Abbey at Prestongrange in East Lothian. The monks needed coal particularly for the saltpans they had established at Preston. The pans were kept boiling day and night. Three gallons of sea water produced a pound of salt. The easily-won coal by the shore was soon exhausted and supplied were carted in from the lands close to Newbattle Abbey via the Salter's Road or Salter's Way. Part of the road still carries this name.

The monks were active traders and had a harbour built at Prestongrange for the export of coal, wool and hides and the import of luxury goods (wines, spices and fine cloth). Newbattle Abbey owned thousands of acres of land and the monks were notably efficient farmers, though the monastic farms would have been largely in the hands of tenant farmers. Rents and tithes were paid in kind (wool, hides, grain, etc.) and delivered to a central place called a grange for storage in granaries and barns. Newton Grange was one of the granges of Newbattle Abbey. The word 'ton' or 'toun' is Anglo-Saxon for farm or township and so Newton Grange means roughly 'The granary at the new farm.'

At the dissolution of the monastries in 1560, the abbot of Newbattle Abbey was Mark Ker, second son of Sir Andrew Ker of Cessford. It's unlikely that he was in fact a monk. The vast wealth of the great monastries had frequently been diverted into private hands and the title abbot was a sinecure. Mark Ker became a Protestant at the Reformation. He took the title of Commendator ('Protector') of Newbattle Abbey and became effective owner of extensive lands in East Lothian, Midlothian, Peebles, Lanark and Fife. Ownership was formally granted in a charter from King James VI to Mark Ker's son in 1587 and a descendent of his became Marquis of Lothian in 1701. The title, and much of the land, have remained in the Ker family right up to the present day.

In those early days, coal was dug in small quantities from drift mines and shallow bell pits. When problems were encountered (roof falls or flooding) the workings were abandoned and another pit or mine was

1

begun. Much of Newbattle parish is riddled with abandoned pits, though mostly there is no visible evidence of their existence. The Rev. John Thomson said in 1839, "There are coal pits and consequently roads leading to them in almost every field." In the mid eighteenth century there were pits at Bryans and Langlaw belonging to the Marquis of Lothian. Langlaw employed seven colliers and Bryans employed thirteen colliers, besides two oncost men, an overseer and two female bearers for carrying down pit props and carrying out redd. The men were paid to deliver the coal to the pithead and generally employed their wives and daughters to carry the coal to creels up wooden stairs to the surface.

By an Act of Parliament in 1606, no coalmaster could hire any colliers or coalbearers without written authority from the master whom they had last served. In effect, collier families were serfs virtually owned by the coalmasters and included in the valuation and sale of collieries. If they ran away, they could be reclaimed and fined (if caught within a year and a day). Parents of new-born children were given a present (arles) by the coal owner, theoritically to bind the child to the colliery. In fact, there was no legal means of enforcing this until that child had worked for a year at the pit, but colliers had neither the knowledge, the means, nor the will to fight such punitive conditions.

There was usually a company shop (called a truck shop or tommy shop) at each colliery. In 1755 the overseer at Bryans Colliery paid the Marquis of Lothian the large sum of £41 a year for the exclusive right to run a truck shop at Bryans. Advances in wages were readily paid to the colliers and the largest part of any advance had to be spent in the company shop where clothes, food, alcohol and hardware goods could be bought and where prices were uncommonly high. A condition of permanent debt was thought to be a good way to oblige men to remain at the pit. More often, it led to colliers doing a 'moonlight flit' to escape increasing debt. Frequently an inducement was offered by a rival coal owner to tempt men to move to their own works.

The truck system was widely criticised and an attempt was made to suppress it by means of the Truck Act of 1831 but it continued long after that.

There was a serious shortage of colliers in the late eighteenth century and, despite high wages, men could not be attracted into the industry because of the taint of bondage. The influential coal owners, therefore, pushed through Acts of Parliament in 1775 and 1799 in an attempt to loosen the ties of bondage and recruit more labour.

The minister of Newbattle had very little sympathy for the colliers. In the First Statistical Account of the parish (1795) he wrote, "Limestone and coals are found in abundance in this parish, the whole of which may be said to be under-laid with them. The coal, particularly, produces every year above £1000 of free profit; and yet we felt as much as many others, the recent scarcity of that necessary article. This evil was not, as some have supported, an effect of the increasing demand. The truth is, that the colliers can earn in three days as much as may support them very fully through the week; they become dissipated and untractable; they insist upon making their own terms; and, if the abuse of that liberty which was lately extended to them, could be admitted as a sufficient reason for abridging it, many restrictions might be suggested which would be useful both to the public and themselves."

Freedom lured away substantial numbers of miners and failed, at first, to attract new recruits into the coalmining industry (times were prosperous due to the Napoleonic War). Substantial bounty payments were therefore made by coal owners to encourage colliers to sign long contracts (up to two years) to work at their pits. The end of the war with France in 1815 led to much unemployment in Britain and made recruitment of men into coal mining much easier.

There was a daily minimum wage for a specified tonnage of coal produced by each man, This was called a darg. the rated fluctuated greatly and could be as little as 2/- a day or as high as 5/- when coal was scarce and demand high. Piece rates were paid after the darg had been reached. Deductions were made for house rent, school fees, lights, tool sharpening and for the doctor. Coal was supplied free but the men had to supply their own tools and provide labour, usually their wives and children, to get the coal to the shaft bottom. Wages were paid fortnightly on 'Pay Friday' and some men never got back to work until Tuesday or Wednesday after that weekend! As a form of insurance in case of sickness many workmen joined Benefit Societies. For an annual subscription of a few shillings a year, a small weekly wage was payable in the event of being off work through illness. Funeral expenses were also paid. The two main local societies were the Langlaw Carter's Friendly Society. The

3

rules were strict – no money was paid for illness "induced through drink," no public houses were to be visited whilst off sick, no spirits were to be taken unless recommended by a doctor and no funeral money was paid for death caused by suicide, debauchery, duelling or law. Membership was restricted to men under 38 years of age.

On the second Friday of July, the Friendly Societies of Newbattle had their annual Play Day when, led by a band, the members in their regaha and carrying banners marched through Easthouses to Dalkeith and then back to Newton Grange via Newbattle. The Play Day was a holiday for the pit and the school children. The procession took place in the morning and for the rest of the day there were 'the shows' to be enjoyed at Newton Grange, dancing on the green and a celebratory meal in the colliery schoolroom in the evening. Collier families in New-battle parish seldom applied for poor relief, generally being able to support their ill or ageing relatives through their own efforts or through their subscription to a Friendly Society.

There was growing public concern in the early nineteenth century about the deplorable living conditions of collier families. There was agitation to ban women and young children from working underground and in 1840 a Parliamentary Commission was set up to review the evidence. Here are some of the submissions made by employees of the Marquis of Lothian.

Mr Gibson, Manager of the East and West Bryants Mines, belonging to the Most Noble Marquis of Lothian: "We employ near 400 persons in the Bryant's mines; 123 are females; about 40 of the males are under 18 years of age, say from 8 to 18; they are chiefly employed at drawing coals on the railroads below. Colliers are not restrained by any agreement here beyond two weeks; on their leaving we give them free lines to any other colliery that they may flit to, on being paid any money we may have advanced. Children are certainly taken down too early; it is a bad picture, but it is the fault of parents themselves."

John Wilson, late overseer to the Newbattle colliery: "I am 66 years of age, and have been 40 years on the Marquis's work; have had 20 children; only 11 in life; have only one son at the coal wall, and he would not have gone but he married a coal-bearer when scarcely 19 years of age. Colliers are more careless, and have more liberty than other tradesmen; they take their children down too early, more from habit than for their use. When both parents are below, they think they prevent them running o'erwild about. Few women here stay at home; they work below until the last hour of pregnancy and often bear the child before they have time to wash themselves. Women go below 10 and 12 days after confinement in many cases. Few coal-wives have still-born children. Accidents are very frequent, more from carelessness than otherwise; no notice is ever taken, for when people are killed they are merely carried out and buried, and there is very little talk about it. Children rarely ever go to school after once down, if they do the fatigue prevents them from acquiring much education. I do not think colliers are better off than they were 46 years ago. I could earn 15s. a week at that time, and it went much farther in the markets. Butcher meat was 2½d. and 3d. per heavy pound, and meal 23s. the load. Colliers have always drank hard; not so much now, as whiskey, their only drink is much dearer.''

John Syme, 16 years old, coal-hewer: "I get two tons of coals down in a day, of the rough coal, which I've 2s. 2d. a ton. I generally work nine and ten days in the fortnight; rarely less than nine. Go to work when it suits me.''

Jane Brown, 13 years old, putter: "Has been wrought 12 months in the East Bryants. My employment is pushing the carts on the iron rails; the weight of coal is the cart is 7 to 8 cwt; a hundred-weight is 100 lbs.; it can't be more. I work 12 hours, and rest a bit when engine stops. I change myself sometimes; when I go to the night-school, not otherwise. I go three times a week; am trying the writing; can't shape many letters at present. Father is dead; mother and four of us work below. The two young ones six years and four years of age, are under care of neighbour, who receives 1s. per week. We have one room in which we all sleep at the East Houses.''

Thomas Duncan, 11 years of age, trapper. "I open the air-doors for the putters; do so from six in the morning till six at night. Mother calls me up at five in the morning and gives me a piece of cake, which is all I get till I return; sometimes I eat it as I gang. There is plenty of water in the pit; the part I am in it comes up to my knees. I did go to school before I was taken down and could read then. Mother has always worked below; but father has run away these five years.''

Medical Return from John Symingston, Esq., Surgeon, Gorebridge, district of Newbattle, Arniston, Mid Lothian: "In reference to the diseases of the adult population in our collieries there is no peculiarity existing amongst them more than in the surrounding population, except in the male, and that consists in the affection of the lungs peculiar to colliers, commonly known by the name of "collier's consumption," attended with black expectoration, which disease generally prevents the collier from continuing his underground operations, almost as soon as other workmen may be reckoned in their prime. Such is the only peculiarity of disease in the collier."

The report was truly horrifying and consequently legislation was passed in 1842 forbidding females of any age and boys under ten years from working underground. Thereafter, ponies were used to haul the hutches of coal underground at the Newbattle pits.

Forty years later, Alexander Mitchell, social reformer and first provost of Dalkeith wrote. "The results of the Act have been most gratifying. The wives and daughters of our colliers now retain no traces of the previous bondage but mingle freely with and in education and deportment are quite equal to the female members of our industrial families. The creel has disappeared from modern life, but man will still remember the ungainly appearance which it gave to them every Saturday as, with bent frame, unsteady step and lack-lustre eye, they tottered homeward bearing in that unsightly hamper the provisions of the week to come."

There was little incentive for Midlothian coal owners to increase production before the mid eighteenth century. Roads were so bad that carts could only be used in summer. In winter, goods (including coal) had to be transported by packhorses carrying loads of one cwt. each. Much better roads into Edinburgh were made after 1750, mainly to enable coal to be more easily transported to the city. Even after that, the insubstantial coal carts carried only twelve to fifteen cwt and the journey from Newbattle to Edinburgh and back took a whole day.

The completion of the Union Canal in 1822 allowed great quantities of coal to be brought from Stirlingshire and places further west to Edinburgh much more cheaply and easily than from Midlothian.

In 1826 the Marquis of Lothian's factor, Mr McGill Rae, wrote to him in alarm about the increased tolls to be charged at Dalkeith. A cart with a ton load would hence forth have to pay 2/- instead of 8d.

Plans were going ahead for a railway to carry Midlothian coal cheaply to the city. The Edinburgh and Dalkeith Railway, with branch lines from Fisherrow and Dalkeith, was completed in 1831. Its southern terminus was at Dalhousie Mains, close to the Newbattle Colliery but separated from it by the river South Esk. The line carried Midlothian coal to Edinburgh and manure back to the country. Later, a passenger service was introduced. It was called the 'Innocent Railway' supposedly because there were never any accidents on the line (although there were accidents). The name may owe more to the fact that its waggons were still horse-drawn long after the steam engine was predominant elsewhere.

Chapter 2

Newton Grange Village – The Beginning

The Newbattle Collieries had expanded enormously since the late 1700s but with the railway to Edinburgh under construction, the Marquis of Lothian invested heavily to increase the output even further. Bryans Pit was deepened and steam-powered winding gear erected. The valley of the South Esk was bridged by a substantial viaduct of wood and stone and private branch lines made to the pits at Bryans and Lingerwood. More men were needed to dig the coal and they had to be housed. Easthouses and Westhouses had always been the main colliery villages but the houses there were old, insanitary and ruinous. In fact, dozens of houses were demolished in these two villages in the 1840s and 1850s and by 1860 Westhouses was derelict and deserted.

Some new houses were built at West Bryans, some at Lingerwood and some at Easthouses, but the majority of new houses were to be constructed on a site opposite Newton Grange Farm. In 1870, during a court case over a right of way dispute, William Romans said, "I remember some collier houses being built at Newton Grange. The second row from Newbattle Road were opposite our old house at Newton Grange. I think the collier houses were built about 1835 and they have been going on increasing ever since."

At the same trial, an old Easthouses residenter, Jane Wilson recalled the place in her early days. "There were few folks at Newton Grange. It was just a farm steading then. Newton Grange was not then built. Easthouses consisted of a good many houses – some 30 or 40."

Between 1835 and 1842, seven parallel rows of sandstone cottages with pantiled roofs were built at Newton Grange on the north side of the colliery railway from Bryans to Dalhousie and at right angles to it. There were 67 houses altogether, costing £34 to £35 each. They were thought to be considerably better than the older collier houses which had only one room, had earth floors and were damp and squalid. Robert Noble, the Newbattle Colliery schoolmaster, commented in 1840, "It is common practice for colliers to keep dung-heaps and dust near the cottage doors and several keep pigs, ducks and poultry in their houses."

Most of the house-building materials were supplied from enterprises belonging to the Marquis of Lothian. Stone came from the sandstone quarry at Masterton and lime was supplied from the limeworks about Westhouses. A brick and tile works was established in 1840 at Newton Grange. The tiles roofed the houses but houses were seldom brick-built until the 1890s.

The Parliamentary Commissioner of 1840, Mr Franks, conducted a further inquiry in 1849 and commented favourably on the houses provided by the Marquis of Lothian, the Duke of Buccleuch and Mr. Ramsay of Whitehill. "The houses are occasionally inspected and those families who neglect the opportunity of living in decency and cleanliness are threatened with dismissal from the works. Excellent gardens are attached to the cottages and also ground for recreation."

Between 1846 and 1851, another 50 houses were built at Newton Grange in five parallel rows to the south of the railway. In 1848 the streets of the village were cleared and drained. Cess pools were put in at every other door. Water was piped into the village and there was a well at the end of each row of houses.

David Bremner, a Scotsman journalist wrote *in 1869, "The Marquis of Lothian owns two hundred and sixty miners' houses, among which are to be found some of the best of the kind in Scotland, together with some of the worst. The Newbattle Colliery, with which they are connected, is one of the oldest in the county, and has never been leased, the successive Marquises keeping the working of it in their own hands. The earlier houses of the miners were miserable thatched hovels; but all the houses built within the past thirty or forty years are of a superior description. The present Marquis, who takes much interest in the welfare of his work-people, commenced a few years ago to work extensive reform in the houses. Only a few cottages of the very old type remain, and the dwellings by which they are being superseded are very comfortable and commodious, some of them containing for or five apartments. The rooms, though small, are lofty and well ventilated. The walls are of brick, the floors of glazed tiles, and the roofs of slate. They are well planned, and externally have some architectural pretensions. All things considered, the houses are well furnished; and it is a noteworthy fact that, though most of the people, while living in the old houses, appeared

*Industries of Scotland, David Bremner.

9

to be careless as to the quality or condition of their furniture, they were no sooner removed into one of those new roomy domiciles than they displayed quite a contrary taste. It is true that some of the new houses appear to be tenanted by people who cannot appreciate the change, yet the foregoing remarks hold good in the majority of cases. The new houses are supplied with water, have flower-gardens in front, and kitchen-gardens and coal houses behind. The rents charged vary from £1 10s. to £3 18s. per annum; and, as elsewhere, the rent is deducted from the fortnightly pay of the men."

The Marquis of Lothian built a school near the village of Newtongrange in 1849, replacing two others he had earlier established at Gallowdeanhill and Easthouses. In fact, there were three schools at Newton Grange: the boys school taught by Mr Noble with 120 pupils (some at night school); a girl's school taught by Miss Dick with 48 pupils; and an infant school taught by Miss Gardner with 73 pupils. The school subjects were Reading, Writing, Grammar, Arithmetic and Bookkeeping. Sewing was available for girls. The fees charged were 1d a month for each subject. A very large number of the collier's children at Newton Grange attended school for at least two or three years. Mr Noble said of those attending evening school that, "their energies being so much exhausted with their daily labour, they all, as soon as they enter school fall into a state of lethergy."

The Marquis of Lothian owned three quarters of the parish of Newbattle but there was one man, John Romans, who owned an isolated seven acres in the midst of the Marquis's property. Jane Wilson of Easthouses recalled, "The farm of Newton Grange belonged to the Marquis but there was one Thomson who owned a bit of it and Johnnie Romans fell heir to Thomson's bit and a two storey house in which they lived."

Johnnie Romans was the joiner and undertaker in Newbattle and his son, also called John, became a successful and prosperous engineer in England. He returned to Scotland in 1863, establishing himself in business in Edinburgh as a gas engineer and coal agent. John Romans was a fervent Scottish Nationalist who later became a J.P. and was elected a County Councillor for Midlothian. He was determined to capitalise on his little empire of seven acres which lay adjacent to Newton Grange - on the north side of the village. Mr Romans planned to build a block of houses and shops on the southern edge of his property, fronting a road called the Loan, which was, however, on the Marquis of Lothian's land. The Marquis decided to close up this road and others in the parish, and John Romans took him to court. He won his case, built his shops and houses and established himself as the collier's champion and constant critic of the Marquis. The colliers called him 'Cocky Romans'. He was so proud of winning the case against the Marquis of Lothian that he had the whole proceedings printed and published as a book to be presented to his friends. No doubt he sent the Marquis a copy too.

One of the shops, on the corner of the Loan and Newbattle Road, was called the 'Abbey Granary'. It was a three storey building with a large statue of a monk on a pedestal high up on one wall. On another wall was a plaque with the inscription, "Praemuim Virtutis Honor. This Building was erected in 1874 on the site where since 1564 had stood the residence of the Lairds of Newton Grange J.R."

The romantic notion that his ancestors were Lairds of Newton Grange is a typical exaggeration of the flamboyant John Romans. Five or six other people had previously owned different parts of the seven acres he had inherited. He certainly could trace his ancestry, through his mother, to a William Junkison who, in 1683, exchanged a small piece of land he owned in Newbattle village for part of a field called Longshot Acres near Newton Grange. The family eventually bought out the other owners and this became John Roman's small estate.

John Romans also built himself an elaborate twentyfour-roomed mansion house in a neo-baronial style on his land. He called it Newton Grange House.

The shops in 'Romans's Buildings' in the Loan were let to a grocer, a draper, a shoemaker and a tailor. The Abbey Granary was run by the Campbell family from 1874 to 1895 as a grocery shop and a short way down the road to Newbattle, at Hope House, was Mr Stone's grocery. There was a post office in Newton Grange from the 1850s and a county police station from the 1840s. Numerous carts, selling butchers meat, bread and groceries, came regularly to the village from Dalkeith, Bonnyrigg and Gorebridge.

A short row of two-storey brick houses was by built the Marquis of Lothian near Newton Grange School in 1871 and more houses were added ten years later under most unusual circumstances. *The Scotsman* of

March 23, 1880, reported as follows: "Cowdenfoot, erected by the Duke of Buccleuch for the miners employed at Dalkeith Colliery, was removed by arrangement with the Marquis of Lothian to a site at the south end of Newton Grange in the parish of Newbattle. When Dalkeith Colliery was dismantled some years ago the miners were employed at Newbattle and have since travelled to work by the train over the colliery's private railway. The houses, of a superior description, are to be re-built as nearly as possible in the same manner, being taken down by sections." This became the village of Cowden Grange until 1898 when Newton Grange was extended and Cowden Grange became part of the new estate of Dean Park. Locals remember it now as the 'Stane Block'.

In 1873, a gasworks had been built by the Marquis of Lothian at New ton Grange and thereafter all the houses had gas lighting, as had Newbattle Church, the Abbey, the colliery School and the colliery office. It had been intended, at first, to provide gas lights for the underground workings but this never happened.

Gas lighting was also supplied to the Church at Newton Grange. The congregation had, at first, a corrugated iron church (built 1874) and then a solid stone building erected in 1880 on land belonging to Mr. Romans. Many miners belonged to the Free Church as opposed to the Church of Scotland ('the Auld Kirk') at Newbattle.

There were two industrial works near Newton Grange. The Dean Oil Works was a firm belonging to Charles Handyside employed in the extraction of oil from coal for industrial purposes. The oil works was situated half a mile south of the village between the Edinburgh road and the main railway line from which they had their own sidings.

The other concern was Robert Craig's Newbattle Paper Mill at Lothian Bridge, which employed 300 people, many of them women. Mr. Craig's lease expired in 1890 and he and the Marquis of Lothian could not agree on conditions for an extension to the lease so he transferred the business to other paper mills he owned, at Caldercruix and Moffat near Airdrie. He took 200 employees with him from Lothian Bridge to Caldercruix. Newbattle Paper Mill was demolished in 1894 but Mr. Craig's fine house, Craigesk, still stands. The closure of the paper mill was a heavy blow to the tradesmen of Newton Grange who lost a lot of business.

Easthouses School, 1890s. This is probably a Sunday School outing about to leave.

Newbattle Paper Mill Label. This beautifully etched view shows the South Esk in the foreground, Craigesk House on the left, a north-bound train on the viaduct with Lothian Bridge Inn on the other side of the viaduct.

Three unknown Newton Grange miners.

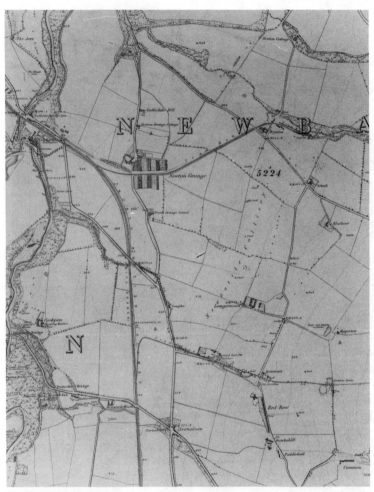

The first Ordnance Survey map of the district, showing the village of Newton Grange in 1854. The Colliery School is to the south. Further south is the Saughs where a creelmaker called Sandy Peacock lived.

Chapter 3

The Sinking of the Lady Vic

Dalkeith Advertiser, 6 March 1890: "THE LOTHIAN COAL COM-
PANY. – The Newbattle Collieries, &c., belonging to the Marquis of
Lothian, and the Whitehill, Dalhousie, and Polton Collieries, &c.,
belonging to Mr. Archibald Hood, have been acquired, and will be
worked on and after Wednesday next, 12th March, the The Lothian
Coal Company (Limited)."

Dalkeith Advertiser, 13 March 1890: "THE LOTHIAN COAL COM-
PANY (LIMITED). - The prospectus of this Company has been issued.
It has been formed for the purpose of acquiring and further developing
the collieries at Newbattle, carried on by the Marquis of Lothian, and
Whitehill, carried on by Mr. Archibald Hood, together with the leases
held by Mr. Hood of the Whitehill and Eldin, Carrington, and Polton
mineral fields, the whole forming an extensive mineral field of nearly
15,000 acres. The purchase consists of the whole plant, including 700
cottages, 600 waggons, buildings, locomotives, and machinery of every
description, also the extensive brick and fireclay works carried on for
many years at Whitehill. The purchase price has been fixed at £200,000,
and the vendors have agreed to take payment of this amount in fully
paid-up Ordinary shares, being the whole present issue of these shares.
There are issued to the public 12,500 5 per Cent. Cumulative Preference shares at £10 each, and these will share ratably in the annual
profits with the Ordinary shares after both have received 5 per cent. The
present output is at the rate of 310,000 tons per annum, but a large
increase is expected after the expenditure of £100,000 on extensions
and improvement, to meet which the capital to be raised by the Preference shares will be applied. At the present rate of output the supply of
coal will last 600 years. After this expenditure, the engineers, Messrs.
M'Creath, Glasgow, and Geddes, Edinburgh, estimate the annual profits at £24,000, while Messrs. William Armstrong & Sons state the same
at £30,000. The chairman of the board of directors is the Marquis of
Lothian, and the managing director is Mr. Hood. The subscription list
will close to-morrow."

There was a great demand for coal in Great Britain in the late 1880s and the price went sky-high as production failed to keep pace with the demand. Many pits throughout the country were being worked out simultaneously, their owners having failed to invest in the opening of new coal seams.

The main partners in the Lothian Coal Co. were Archibald Hood, who became managing director, and the Marquis of Lothian, who was chairman for the first ten years. Archibald Hood was a colliery entrepreneur with business interests in Wales and Scotland. He had leased the Whitehill coalfield from Robert Wardlaw Ramsay of Whitehill in 1856 and, over a number of years, added the leases of adjoining coalfields belonging to three other proprietors, the Earl of Rosebery, Robert Dundas of Arniston and the Earl of Dalhousie.

It was estimated that £100,000 would be needed to create a modern pit at Newton Grange and to build houses for additional workers. The sinking of the shaft at the new pit took four years and was completed in November 1894. It was 1,650 feet deep and was one of the deepest in Scotland. The shaft reached the Lower Coal measures giving access to vast reserves of coal, the upper coal measures being largely worked out.

The pithead workings were completed by 1895 and comprised an extensive range of new buildings with the most up-to-date machinery. Large railway sidings were built with direct access to the main Edinburgh to London railway line.

"The sinking and fitting of the Lady Victoria pit at Newbattle colliery which began in 1890, inaugurated a new era in mineral developments in the two counties (Mid and East Lothian). From every point of view the colliery was one of the best equipped in Scotland." (Andrew Cunningham, Mining in Mid and East Lothian, 1925). The Lothian Coal Company were amongst the earliest in Scotland to generate their own electricity and provide electric light underground. They also experimented with compressed air coal cutters in 1890 and electric coal cutters in 1895.

The new pit was called the Lady Victoria Colliery after Lady Victoria Scott, eldest daughter of the Duke of Buccleuch and wife of the chairman of the Lothian Coal Company, Schomberg Henry Ker, 9th Marquis of Lothian. the miners have always known it as 'the Lady Vic' or just 'the Lady'.

The opening of the Lady Vic was not, however, an altogether happy affair. Coal production elsewhere in Britain had caught up with demand, prices had dropped and wages had been substantially reduced. The daily minimum wage had fallen from 5/- in 1892 to 3/- in May 1893. It rose to 3/6 in August, but a claim for 4/6 a day was refused in October 1893 to the anger of the men, who decided to take action. A series of one day strikes was planned by the union, the Mid and East Miners Association.

The 700 men at the three Newbattle pits (East and West Bryans and Dixon's) took Wednesday 1st November off and the next day the first shift was locked out by the management. The lockout lasted nine weeks. The 1/- a day (which had been granted elsewhere) was offered to the men but only on condition that they worked an eleven day fortnight instead of the usual ten days. The men refused. The other Midlothian miners paid a levy of 2/- a head each week to support them and from the funds accumulated the Newbattle men got 8/- a week, plus 1/- extra for each child under thirteen. A fair number of men left Newbattle to work elsewhere. At the end of the year a compromise was reached. the 1/- rise was awarded and the men agreed to take their idle days at different times and keep a shift of men at work on alternate Saturdays.

In June 1894 the colliery owners throughout Mid and East Lothian notified the men of a reduction from 4/6 a day to 3/6. At a mass meeting in Dalkeith the miners voted by 3203 votes to 230 to strike for no reduction. The strike was long and bitter and there were angry and violent incidents on picket lines. After 17 weeks the men went back. They had to accept the reduction and got no guarantee that there would be no further reductions.

Early in 1895 the Lothian Coal Company reduced the pay to 3/- a day and made an eleven day fortnight compulsory. Elsewhere in Midlothian a ten day fortnight still prevailed.

Thorough research by Mike Cotterill and Colin Denovan on behalf of the Scottish Mining Museum has revealed that the minute books and account books of the Lothian Coal Company have been lost or destroyed. Such information as has been discovered about the early days of the company comes mainly from newspaper reports and other sources researched by Messrs. Cotterill and Denovan. The Dalkeith Advertiser carried reports of most of the earliest annual general meetings of the company, but not 1890 - 1895 nor 1897. Details of share ownership, summaries of current accounts and other details from 1908 onwards had to be lodged with the Board of Trade and are available for study.

The following is part of the Lothian Coal Co. Annual Report of 1895-96.

Dalkeith Advertiser, 29 October 1896: "The year has been very free from labour troubles and accidents, the only important interruptions to work having arisen from want of orders owing to the depressed state of the coal market. Since the date of last report, the output from the Lady Victoria Pit, which then was about 500 tons a day, had increased to about 800 tons a day, the quality of the coals continuing to be satisfactory. Before the tonnage from this pit could be much further increased, it would be necessary to obtain houses for the additional miners who were required to develop the output, the Company's present accommodation being fully occupied, and there being no available dwellings within convenient distance of the colliery. A building company was in process of being formed to erect workmen's houses, a sufficient number of which were to be leased by the company. The Chairman, in moving the adoption of the report, said that the coal trade during the past year had been in a very depressed condition. Many companies had suffered large losses, and some had suffered so much than they had been obliged to shut up altogether. Considering the position of the Lothian Coal Company, it was satisfactory to say that this Company had been able to show a profit on the year. The directors felt great regret that they were unable to declare a divided, but they could not do so until they had altogether wiped out the debit balance, which they hoped to do next year."

The profit that year was £8,000 and this had risen to £19,000 by 1897 - 1898, which was the Lothian Coal Company's best year up till then. The chairman stated that, "In consequence of the strike in Wales, the coal trade in Scotland had shown considerable activity, though it had not done them very much good..." A wage increase at the company's pits had meant, "additional and unavoidable expenditure of many thousand pounds." 1899-1900 was an even better year with profits of £44,500.

The company set up by the Lothian Coal Co. in 1896 to build houses at Newton Grange was the Newbattle and Whitehill Building Co. The first houses in a scheme called Dean Park were completed in 1898 at a cost of £12,000 - approximately £128 a house. A further 93 houses were finished in 1899 and 1900 as part of a large scheme named Monkswood. The population of Newton Grange and Cowden Grange doubled in ten years from 1,210 in 1891 to 2,406 in 1901.

Census Returns

Year	Newton Grange	Cowden Grange
1843	220§	
1851	*	
1861	787	
1871	677	
1881	1010	
1891	957	253
1901	2406	**

§ contemporary estimate
* no recorded figure
** recorded with Newton Grange

There were a number of societies springing up in the village and some amenities had been established. A park had been made in the field on the south side of the village. There was a cricket team, a junior football team, a cycling club, whippet racing, and quoiting. The village had a district nurse (from 1889) and a new school near the Bryans (built 1893). The old colliery schools then became the Lothian Halls which were used for village meetings, concerts, displays and dances. Newton Grange had its own brass band, an annual flower show, an amateur dramatic society and a Burns Club. Other organisations in the village included the Newbattle Girls Friendly Society, the Good Templars' Lodge and the Lothian Lodge of Scottish Mechanics.

The history of licensed houses in Newbattle parish prior to the opening of Newton Grange's two pubs at the end of the nineteenth century is the subject of the next chapter.

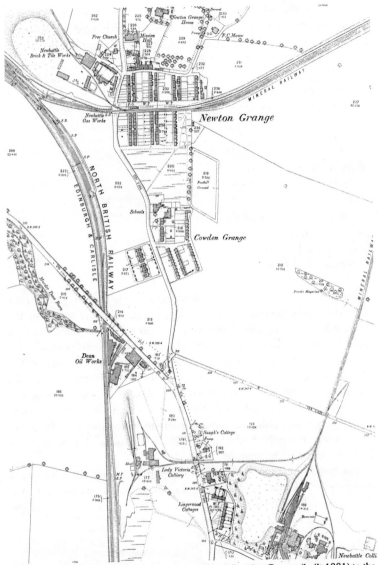

1894 map of Newton Grange showing the village of Cowden Grange (built 1881) to the south.

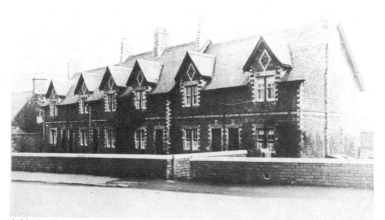

A block of six houses built in 1872 by the Lothian Coal Co. Originally part of Cowden Grange, it then became part of Monkswood and finally, in 1912, became part of St. Davids.

Part of Deanpark, the oldest of the Lothian Coal Company building schemes. It was begun in 1898.

The Peth.

Newbattle Abbey, former home of the Marquises of Lothian, now a residential adult education college.

Newtongrange House, former home of 'Cocky' Romans, self-styled Laird of Newton Grange. Now demolished.

Chapter 4

Early Drinking Houses in Newbattle Parish

The minister of Newbattle parish, Rev. John Thomson, wrote in 1839, "There are five public, or rather dram houses in the parish; and their effects upon the lower orders of society are of the most demoralising nature. There were lately more, but they were fortunately suppressed, and the writer is most anxious to have them still farther reduced."

The five dram-houses were kept by William Stevenson, Newbattle; James Buchan, Easthouses; Widow Drylaw, Stobhill and Mrs Watt, Peaseflatt Mains. Mr. Stevenson was proprietor of the Dambrig Inn at Newbattle where the legendary Camp Meg's* funeral wake took place in 1827. It was always said that much drunken revelry took place on that occasion but the undertaker's son, John Romans, denied it, saying that his father would not have tolerated it nor would the publican, Mr. Stevenson, "a man who was an elder of the kirk session for upwwards of thirty years, and who would permit no drunkenness." As was the custom then, Camp Meg being on the poor roll, the church paid for refreshments after the funeral, i.e. whisky and shortbread.

There were four public houses in Newbattle village at the beginning of the nineteenth century. Besides the Dambrig, there was the Sign of the Sun Inn. The Sign of the Sun building still stands, opposite the Abbey gates. It dates from 1697 and had also been a brewery. The sun was the symbol used by the Marquis of Lothian's family.

Another public house licence was granted to George Liddell at Parkfoot, Newbattle, in 1840 but that was withdrawn in 1857. The number of licences in Easthouses was the subject of a letter to the Marquis of Lothian from his factor. "I am sorry the Minister (Mr. Thomson) here has given a new Certificate of Character to Mitchell at Easthouses, which is a primary step to obtain the whisky licence; in consequence of this it will occasion me some considerable trouble to put a stop to it. He is perfectly aware there are besides three Public Houses in that village. I

*Camp Meg was a strange old lady, a skilled horse doctor, who lived in an isolated cottage of the Camp Hill above Newbattle.

hope however to get it suppressed by the Justices at the general meeting."

The minister referred to by Mr. McGill Rae was the same Mr. Thomson who spoke out so severely against the number of public houses in the parish a few years later. Mr Mitchell did get his licence and that made four public houses in Easthouses for a time.

The J.P.s were keen to suppress licences in Midlothian in an attempt to curb drinking and drunkenness and two of the Easthouses pubs were closed in 1829 and another (Mitchell's) in 1831. The remaining one was run by the Buchan family (who were also farmers) until 1860. Thereafter, there was no pub at Easthouses until 1946 when Andrew Aikman opened the Barley Bree.

Though public house licences were generally being suppressed, licences for inns on turnpike roads were being granted. An inn was built beside the main road from Edinburgh to Selkirk near Dalhousie Mains by the Marquis of Lothian beside the main road from Edinburgh to Selkirk near Dalhousie Mains. It was called the Lothian Bridge Inn and it keep their horses overnight or they could rent a horse and exchange it for a fresh mount at another inn further along the road.

Between 1838 and 1847, the Royal Mail coach from Edinburgh to London travelled past the Lothian Bridge Inn twice daily in each direction but it never stopped. It stopped only at the White Hart Inn, Dalkeith, which was the post office for Newbattle parish. the next stop was at Fushiebridge Inn where the first change of horses took place. This was also a post office. The roads were crowded with traffic but the stage coach was supreme. Speed was all important and at the height of the coaching boom London could be reached from Edinburgh in under thirty hours.

The innkeeper at Lothian Bridge from the beginning was John Stobbs. He was also the blacksmith at Lothian Bridge and after he died this business passed into the hands of the Kirkwood family who were reknowned agricultural implement makers. John Stobbs was succeeded as innkeeper by his widow, Annes. She retired in 1867 and went to live with her daughter, a minister's wife in Newton Stewart.

By this time the heyday of coaching was long past. The railways took over the long-distance journeys from the coaches and the licensing courts began to suppress inn licences. The Lothian Bridge Inn was closed by the Marquis of Lothian in 1867 when Mrs. Stobbs left. For two years there were no licensed premises in Newbattle Parish. In 1869 two grocers at opposite ends of the parish (at Whitehill and Hunterfield) were granted licences to sell ale and porter.

The central and most populous part of the parish was totally 'dry'. The Marquis of Lothian refused to allow the sale of drink on any premises belonging to him and he owned almost all the houses. Thirsty miners had to walk about two miles to the Justinlees Inn at Eskbank or a mile and a half in the other direction to Newtonloan Toll, where there were two licensed grocers. Both had been public houses until the 1850s when stricter licensing laws had obliged them to stop selling drink for consumption on the premises. This led to the custom of men drinking by the roadside outside licensed grocers. It was a widespread habit and the police found it difficult to stop. Surreptitious drinking also took place in certain back shops right up to recent times.

Sandy Fairlie tells of an incident that befell two brothers from Gorebridge at Beveridges of Newtonloan Toll in his lively book 'Early Coal Mining in Arniston and Newbattle'. "For instance, might I relate the occasion when Rob Young had an infant who died and he arranged with his brother Sandy to carry the box, as they called it, down to Newbattle churchyard. Well, off they set for their long walk; on reaching Newton Loan Toll licensed grocers, they decided to have a rest and a dram, so, placing the box on the dyke, they settled down to have their dram, and maybe had a few more drams, so much so that when they again resumed their journey they forgot all about the box, and were quite a mile down the road when Sandy said to Rob, "Where's the box"? "Oh", he says, "I clean forgot all about it." On returning to the toll they recovered it unharmed apart from the fact that it had fallen down at the back o' the dyke. Resuming their journey and arriving at the Kirkyard a bit late, they received a lecture from Auld Wull, the gravedigger, for keeping him waiting. The unpleasantness was soon overcome after the box had been lowered into its resting place and the bottle produced; the dram, as it were, gave them a sort of peace of mind."

John Romans, joiner and undertaker in Newbattle, retired to Newton Grange Cottage, one of a handful of houses on the seven acres he owned just north of Newton Grange village. He decided to seek a licence for a public house in 1850 but his application was refused.

There was a brewery cart from Archibalds of Dalkeith which delivered barrels of beer around the Newbattle district occasionally -but mainly to farmers. They would order beer or ale for their harvest workers who were provided with their meals at harvest time as part of their wages. It was standard to provide a couple of pints of beer per person with each meal.

John Roman's son had built shops and houses on his land at Newton Grange and one of his tenants was John Campbell, who had a grocery at the Abbey Granary. Mr. Campbell applied for, and was granted, a licensed grocers' certificate in 1880, the first Newton Grange licence. At the same licensing court a Mrs. Reid who also had a grocers shop in Newton Grange was refused a licence to sell table beer.

Dalkeith Advertiser, 1st May 1893: "OPEN-DRINKING AT NEWTONGRANGE. SIR, - Permit me to call attention through your columns to what is growingly felt to be a public nuisance and disgrace in the village of Newton Grange. There is unfortunately a licensed grocer in the place, and in its vicinity there gather crowds of men, young and old, every other week, who do their drinking in the open street to the great inconvenience of the neighbours and to the demoralisation of their children. No later than Monday week last the scenes witnessed there were nothing less than a disgrace to a respectable community. It is a hardship for those disturbed by the brawling of these revelers and heartbreaking that their children should have to hear and witness such scenes. The best cure would be to have the license withdrawn from the place, but, failing this, let me appeal to those who indulge to have respect to their neighbours' comfort and the children's weal, and if they still feast in this ugly form, let it be in their own homes. The moral sense of the community is recoiling against this thing, and what is needed is that every respectable inhabitant should shun the corner and raise a strong protest against the practice. - Yours, &c, A VILLAGE WELL-WISHER."

There was an active temperance movement in Newton Grange going back to 1872 when the Good Templar Lodge 'Lothian Star' was founded. They built their own hall on land sold to one of their members by John Romans. By then, they had 67 adult members and 97 juvenile members. Other temperance organisations in the village included the United Free Church Total Abstinence Society, the Independent Order of Rechabites, the Sons of Temperance and the Band of Hope.

Dalkeith Advertiser, 21 February 1895: "THE LICENSING QUES-
TION AT NEWBATTLE. SIR - Public opinion in Newbattle at present
is greatly exercised on the subject of licensing, and a very general cry is
being raised that a certain license should be abolished. There can be no
denial that a great number of people, unfortunately, take more strong
drink than is good for them, and thus impoverish both themselves and
their families. An effort has been made in certain quarters in this district
to remedy this evil, with, I believe, a great amount of success. The teetotal party argue that to stop licenses would also be to stop drinking.
Possibly it would be a certain extent, but I fear not entirely, and by closing legitimate trade and so introduce new evils. Nearly every person
agrees that private individuals by the operation of laws intended for the
benefit of the people as a whole. To prevent this I would suggest that if a
licensed house is to be allowed it should be conducted in such a way that
the profits would be applied to the public benefit. Already many of the
people obtain their provisions from one or other of the co-operative
stores, where the profits are divided amongst the members. Why should
a licensed shop not be conducted on the same principles? As property in
the Newbattle is almost entirely in the hands of Marquis of Lothian or
the Lothian Coal Company, they, as landlords, could make their own
conditions, and I would suggest that if such a scheme were adopted that
a very stringent clause be introduced in the lease binding the management to the orderly conduct of the business, under a penalty of having
their lease cancelled at short notice by the landlord. The committee of
management could be selected in a similar way to a co-operative store
committee, and the members would have control of the business. I do
not suggest that such a business be run for the purpose of doing a large
trade, but rather that the management, having full control, could see as
to quality, and if necessary give instructions that certain people should
not be supplied on any terms. There should be no objection to temperance men acting on the management; indeed they should be
welcomed, and thus they would have a voice in controlling what they
considered improper. Any profits from such a business could be applied
to any local scheme of usefulness, the benefits of which would be open
to all, whether members of the shop or not. Perhaps, Mr. Editor, you
might open your columns to the discussion of such a scheme. I am,
&c., NEMO"

Dalkeith Advertiser, 28 February 1895: 'PUBLIC MEETING - A public meeting called by the Newbattle kirk session "to consider the question of a licensed house in Newton Grange" was held in the Old School there last Thursday evening, and there was a very large attendance of householders and heads of families. The Rev. J.C. Carrick presided, and all the members of session were present. A long discussion was taken part in, and at the close a vote of those present was taken for or against a licensed grocer, a licensed public-house, or no license at all, when it was unanimously carried that, in the opinion, of the meeting, the license should be done away with altogether. A committee was appointed to take steps to petition against the transfer and the license."

Rumours were circulating in Newton Grange in 1895 that Mr Romans was about to let the Abbey Granary to someone other than Mrs. Campbell, who had held the license since her husband's death in 1880. Many of the villagers were angered by Mr. Roman's action and supported Mrs. Campbell but the temperance movement chose this moment to campaign vociferously for the abolition of the licence altogether.

Mrs. Campbell's lease ended at Whitsun, 1895 and Mr. Romans refused to renew it. Instead he let the shop to Alexander Henderson, an Edinburgh man who subsequently was granted the licence, despite strong opposition at the licensing court meeting.

Mrs. Campbell was very angry at Mr. Roman's treatment of her and felt she had not had a fair hearing at the licensing court. She took the unusual stop of sending a copy of all the letters which had passed between herself and Mr. Romans during the previous six months to the *Dalkeith Advertiser*. The entire correspondence was published, being described as having been "supressed at the recent Licensing Court when the licence was transferred to another."

Mr. Romans initially intimated a 50% rent increase for the Abbey Granary, asking for £85 a year instead of £57. He said he had frequently been offered twice the rent Mrs. Campbell paid for a five year lease. In reply, Mrs. Campbell stated that £57 was the maximum she could pay as business had declined since Craig's Paper Mill had closed and the recent miner's strike had affected trade. She admitted that the sinking of the new shaft by the Lothian Coal Company had helped her business but since it was finished takings had fallen considerably.

Mr. Romans was not impressed and increased his demands. This is an extract from his third letter: "I will agree to grant you a lease of ten years of the premises, on condition that you pay me £500 in cash at the term of Whitsun next, the date of the new lease. I agreeing to provide and fix in the premises one high pressure boiler with kitchen range, a bath with hot and cold water, with all the necessary fitments, and also a patent water closet complete."

This was clearly a preposterous demand and was firmly rejected by Mrs. Campbell who said "I could for the same sum build a house with all the latest improvements." She offered £70 a year which was refused and she failed to answer any of his final three letters, which had become rather hostile.

Chapter 5

The Newton Grange Licensing Question

There were three applications for licences in Newton Grange before the Midlothian Licensing Court at Whitsun 1897. The applicants were Alexander Henderson, for a public house licence at the Abbey Granary; James Hood, general manager of the Lothian Coal Company, for a public house licence "near the railway crossing, Newton Grange", and Thomas Stewart, grocer, for a licence to sell alcohol from his shop at Hope House. Objections were made by Newbattle Free Church Deacon's Court to Mr. Henderson's and Mr. Stewarts' applications but not to Mr. Hood's. References were made in court to this discrepancy and it was suggested that there may have been a connection between the fact that Mr. Callender, secretary of the Lothian Coal Company, was also a deacon of Newbattle Free Church.

Petitions were produced against the licences (253 signatures) and in favour (314 signatures). There were four main points made against the applications.

1) There had been no licence in the village before 1880.
2) There were two licensed premises "within ten minutes walk" of Newtongrange.
3) There was widespread opposition.
4) It would cause disorderly and unseemly scenes.

Counsel for the Lothian Coal Company mentioned the large population of the village (2,500)* and that there were 100 houses being built. The public house would be an adaptation of the Gothenburg system, two workmen would be on the management committee and profits would be used for raising an accident fund or "promoting healthful recreation." It was pointed out that the nearest licensed premises (at Eskbank and Newtonloan) were one and a half miles distant (thirty to fortyfive minutes's walk – not ten minutes, as the opposition stated).

The court voted in favour of a second licence (28 for, 8 against) and,

*This was incorrect. The combined population of Newton Grange and Cowden Grange was 1,210 in 1891 and it was about the same in 1897.

for Mr. Henderson's application rather than Mr. Hood's (23 for, 10 against). Mr Stewart was granted a licence unanimously. So for the first time there was a pub in Newton Grange. Mr. Henderson called it the Abbey Inn. There was also a licensed grocer's shop nearby at Hope House. Both licenced premises were on Mr. Romans' property.

The Lothian Coal Company had intended to run their public house, if granted a licence, on an adaption of the Gothenberg system, which needs some explanation.

In the early nineteenth century, Sweden was awash with legally - produced home-made brandy. There were 170,000 licensed stills in a country with a population of under three million. Every householder had an absolute right to distill their own spirits. The annual consumption of spirits per head of population was 7½ gallons. Drunkenness was a national scandal and in 1855 a law was passed making domestic distilling illegal. The local authorities were given powers to grant licences and the city of Gothenburg pioneered a new system which was to provide a model for municipal authorities throughout Sweden and Norway. All the retail spirit licences in Gothenburg were awarded to one company, a trust, which was to run pubs, off licences and restaurants in a manner that would not encourage excessive spirit drinking. The premises were to be clean but not attractive, the employees would have no interest in pushing spirit sales to make a profit and the holders of shares in the company were limited to a 5% annual return on their money. All profits above that were to go to the town treasury and used to benefit the local community through the provision of parks, libraries, museums, etc). Despite the fact that beer and wine sales were excluded from this system it was extremely profitable and yielded thousands of pounds a year to the city of Gothenburg.

The idea caught on rapidly in Sweden and each municipality adapted the system to suit their own purposes. The fame of the system spread and the idea was taken up by public house reformers and temperance compaigners in Britain - Scotland in particular. Around the turn of the century several public house trusts were set up in such places as Peebles, Leven, Clydebank, Broxburn and Tranent but the idea of controlling public houses and spending the profits of the community caught on most dramatically with the coal companies in Central Scotland.

The Lothian Coal Company applied to Midlothian Licensing Court for a public house licence in Newton Grange for a second time in 1899. This time the application was made by their nominee, a disabled ex-miner called Andrew Anderson, who would be the manager if the licence was granted.

Counsel for the applicants, Mr Crabbe Watt, made a lengthy case on their behalf. He stated that there was only one public house and one licensed grocer in the village, though the population was rapidly expanding. One hundred houses had been recently built, a hundred more were soon to be erected and within a few years three hundred more would go up. A petition in favour of the licence had 430 signatures. Profits would not be retained by the company but would be used to benefit the whole community. The Hill of Beath Tavern, established by the Fife Coal Company, was cited as a successful example of this type of public house management. There, electricity had been supplied to the village using the tavern profits and a bowling green had been provided.

In answer to a question Mr. Crabbe Watt stated that "there would be a balance sheet issued and a public audit of accounts."A letter was read out from the Marquis of Lothian supporting the application and withdrawing any restriction against granting of a licence on his feu. The Chief Constable thought there was room for another public house in Newton Grange.

A petition against the granting of a licence to the Lothian Coal Company was ridiculed, having only seven signatories. Two of these had withdrawn their opposition, one had denied signing and the other four were tenants of Mr. Roman's son.

Mr. C.D. Murray, advocate, opposed the licence application. He thought the premises were unsuitable for a public house being converted from two adjacent dwelling houses. He criticised Mr. Anderson, saying he had no experience in the licensed trade and was disabled. Mr. Murray further stated that the Lothian Coal Company should not be running a public house as it put them in danger of breaking the intentions of the Truck Act (an Act designed to prevent companies selling goods to their employees). He thought the coal company should form a club if they wished to benefit their employees. On three previous occasions, officials of the Lothian Coal Company had petitioned against a licence being granted in Newton Grange.

Mr. Romans, as a J.P. and member of the licensing court, wished to speak against the licence. The chairman felt that he should not take part in the debate as he was owner of the Abbey Inn and an interested party but Mr. Romans insisted on his right to speak. His point was that the members of the licensing court who were also shareholders of the Lothian Coal Company should not vote. Mr. Roman's objection was overruled.

The licence as approved by 19 votes to 10. Three shareholders in the Lothian Coal Company voted in favour and Mr. Romans voted against.

A fortnight later, at a further licencing court meeting to confirm licences granted, the same arguments were brought up for and against. Mr. Murray, advocate for the objectors, declared that, because the Lothian Coal Company shareholders had voted for the licence application made by their company, the decision of the licencing court was invalid and should not be confirmed. Four voted for confirmation of the licence, Colonel Wardlaw Ramsay, Sir John Cowan (both shareholders in the Lothian Coal Co.), Colonel Trotter and Sir James Gibson Craig and two voted against, Mr. Corstorphine and Mr. Blaik.

The two J.P.s who had voted against the licence, Alexander Corstorphine of Juniper Green and David Blaik of Gorebridge, along with two Newton Grange objectors, J.C. Blaik and J.W. Armitstead, raised an action in the Court of Session against Andrew Anderson and the JPs who had voted for the licence.

Mr. Armitstead and Mr. J.C. Blaik were both shopkeepers in the Loan and claimed to have suffered discomfort and annoyance "by the granting of the licence for premises near to their own".

Dalkeith Advertiser, 22 June 1899: "The pursuers aver that the granting of the certificate was illegal, the premises unsuitable (being workmen's houses), the applicant, Anderson, had no experience, the licence was unnecessary and the Company had hitherto opposed the granting of licences in the village. They further aver that the defenders, Sir John Cowan, D.J. Macfie and Colonel Wardlaw Ramsay, were disqualified from acting at the said licensing meetings by law and were liable for each offence to a penalty of £50, they being proprietors or tenants of house or premises for which such certificate was applied for and granted."

Sir John Cowan had 490 shares in the Lothian Coal Co, Mr Macfie had 410 and Colonel Wardlaw Ramsay had 100. Sir John Cowan also had 50 shares in the Newbattle and Whitehill Building Co. (a subsidiary company of the Lothian Coal Co. and owners of the Dean Tavern premises) and was a director of both companies.

Lord Darling reserved judgement and, as the licence was still valid, the Dean Tavern opened for business on October 20th, 1899. A management committee had been formed for the Dean by the Lothian Coal Co., which nominated three members - James Hood, general manager, John Callender, company secretary and Mungo Mackay, manager of Newbattle Colliery. Two workmen had been elected at a public meeting in the village - James Taylor and William Pryde. Both were active in the running of local Friendly Societies. This was the only time an election was held. Subsequently, vacancies for workmen's representatives were always filled on the nomination of the rest of the committee. James Gilmour, wages clerk at the pit, was appointed clerk and treasurer to the committee at £12 a year.

Meantime the case in the Court of Session was continuing and in December Lord Stormonth Darling ruled that the licence was invalid as three shareholders in the Lothian Coal Co. were on the licensing court bench and had voted for the licence which had been granted to that company.

The Dean Tavern Committee resolved to appeal against this decision and business continued meantime. *Dalkeith Advertiser*, 12th April 1900: "THE DEAN TAVERN - At a meeting of the Committee of Management of the Dean Tavern, Newton Grange, held on Tuesday night, the balance sheet, for the period from its opening to 31st March, as audited by Messrs Howden & Molleson C.A., was submitted. The balance sheet which had been prepared to produce to the court on the occasion of the application for a renewal of the licence, in accordance with the promise made to the last licensing court, showed an available profit, as the result of the five month's working, of £175 17s. As only the highest class of liquors has been sold and that at moderate prices the committee deemed the result highly satisfactory. The committee took into consideration the object to which this profit should be applied, and being informed that there was a general desire among the inhabitants for a public bowling green, it was resolved to lay aside this sum and as much of the future profit as would be required for that purpose."

The balance sheet had been prepared to present to the Midlothian Licensing Court in support of Andrew Anderson's application for the renewal of the Dean licence. Lord Darling had not yet ruled whether there were sufficient grounds in law to carry an appeal to the Inner House and the committee decided to make two licence applications. One application was made for the renewal of the existing licence and one for a new licence for other premises in case the court case was lost.

Dalkeith Advertiser: 19th April, 1900 "On the suggestion of the Chairman, when the application of Andrew Anderson, Dean Tavern, Newton Grange, on behalf of the Lothian Coal Co. Ltd. for a public house licence, came up, all the members of the Court who had shares in either the Coal Company or Whitehill Building Co. Ltd. left the bench"

New petitions were produced. The Dean Tavern committee had organised one and that had attracted 353 signatures. Another petition for the objectors had but 9 signatures, including that of the Abbey Inn's manager, the barman and the potboy. Mr. Cooke, representing the licence applicants alleged that the four gentlemen who had brought the action in the Court of Session against the granting of the licence were, in fact, representing the Licensed Trade Defence Association.

Mr Young, on behalf of the objectors, said that "to give a licence to a company in the position of the Lothian Coal Company would be to enable it to take back from its employees, in the price of excisable liquor, the money which had been given to them as wages. That was a result to be avoided, because it was plainly open to abuse. It would also be opposed to the interests of free and fair trade, because a company which had exceptional means of directing the custom of their employees should not be encouraged and assisted to come into unfair competition with the ordinary individual trader." There was applause in the court at this statement but it was immediately suppressed.

Mr. Robert Brown, JP, a miners union leader, supported the application and assured Mr. Young that the employees were quite capable of looking after themselves. He could testify that the community was nearly unanimous in favour of the licence. Another JP, in favour, remarked that the employees "were not yet under the thumb of the employers."

The licence was granted by 24 votes to 7.

Lord Stormonth Darling made his decision on the so-called "Gothenburg Experiment" in the Court of Session on May 29th, 1900. The case had hinged on the fact that three Lothian Coal Co. shareholders had voted for the Dean Tavern licence at the Licensing Court in April, 1899. As the licence had been re-granted at the Whitsun Licensing Court on April 17th 1900, and the Coal Co. shareholders had taken no part in the voting, Lord Darling held that the licence was valid.

Expenses in the original action had been granted to the pursuers (the two J.P.s and Mr. Armitstead and Mr. Blaik). So the Lothian Coal Co. had to pay for that, as well as their own expenses. Lord Darling refused to grant expenses in the appeal case and each party was responsible for their own expenses. The Dean Tavern Committee had an account for £151-4-7 from their solicitors, Anderson and Chisholm, and this was paid out of the first years profits of the Dean.

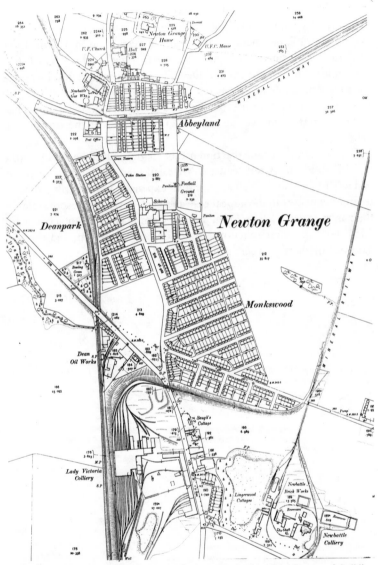

1907 map showing the results of the first nine years of the Lothian Coal Company's building programme.

1914. Housing had now reached the company railway line. Part of Monkswood has been re-named First to Sixth Street.

Part of the Square (built 1914). These larger houses were for colliery officials. In later years the Square deteriorated and got a bad name locally.

The company railway level crossing was called the White Gates. The S.M.T. bus in the centre is fuelled by gas held in a huge balloon on the roof.

Abbeyland viewed from the public park. This was the original village of Newtongrange. Romans's building can be seen on the right of the picture.

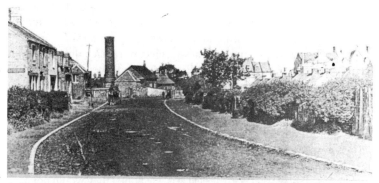

A view of the bottom end of the village, looking along Main Street. The gasworks chimney is on the left and Abbeyland is on the right. The colliery railway line to the gasworks and the redd bing crossed the street just past the horse and cart.

Chapter 6

The Lothian Coal Company: 1900-1920

1901 was a good year for the Lothian Coal Co. but for the following five years demand for coal was poor and prices low. There was a tax on coal exports and this affected the Coal Co. as it exported a lot of coal to the Continent. The company was tempted to reduce wages but since 1899 wages had been controlled nationally by a Conciliation Board composed of coal owners and miners. The profit for the year 1903 -1904 was £10,000. One of the directors commented at the A.G.M. that "the balance is a miserable affair, considering the large amount of capital in the company. The company has done much for the comfort of the workers and the workers in return ought to do all they could for the company." (*Dalkeith Advertiser*, 6 October 1904)

Other ways were sought to reduce production costs and in 1905 electric coal cutting machinery was introduced to Newbattle Colliery and this increased output and cut the average cost of coal production. That year, the great seam was reached. It was six feet of excellent steam coal and good household coal. Newbattle Colliery was noted for the quality of its cannel coal which was particulary suitable for the manufacture of gas and was in demand in London, Europe and America.

In 1907 work was begun on a new project to replace the old Bryans Pit. A drift mine was developed at Easthouses and when opened it 1910 Bryans Pit was closed.

1907 was a good year for business and the minimum wage rose to 7/6 a day, though it fell back the following year. Part of the Dalkeith Advertiser report of the chairman's speech at the 1908 A.G.M. went as follows "The advance of the rate of wages was more serious for them than the mere increase of wages, for they always found that when colliers had high wages they worked a great deal less. He hoped they would not have that difficulty to contend with now that the wages were back to 6/3. They had no fear of the exhaustion of the collieries; coal would last for many more generations, and that was another reason why they were anxious to build houses, and build them substantially, and tempt the workmen by giving good accommodation." (*Dalkeith Advertiser*, 24 October 1908)

1909 and 1910 were good years for the company with profits around £20,000 each year and wage rates quite low.

On the outbreak of war in 1914 many miners enlisted and coal production fell as a result. The government brought out a Coal Emergency Act and took control of the coal industry. Minimum wage rates rose continuously and at the end of the war they stood at 13/- a day. There was a coal famine with huge demand at home and abroad. At this time the miner's leaders demanded that wages should be increased by 3/6 a day, that the working day should be reduced from eight to six hours and that collieries should be nationalised. The Coal Controller, on the advice of the coal owners offered 1/- a day. A national strike was imminent and a Royal Commission was hastily set up under the chairmanship of Sir John Sankey. Of the twelve members, six were miners representatives and three represented the coal owners. The main recommendations of the Sankey Commission were: (1) An immediate increase of 2/- a day, (2) The introduction of a seven hour day, (3) Nationalisation of the pits as from 1922 and (4) One penny per ton of coal produced to be set aside to provide amenities in mining areas.

Three of these recommendations were accepted and acted upon. Only the one concerning nationalisation was rejected.

The massive housebuilding programme of the Lothian Coal Co. begun in 1896 had continued into the twentieth century. Between 1901 and 1914 another 350 houses were built at Newtongrange in the schemes of Dean Park, St. David's and Monkswood by the Newbattle and Whitehill Building Co. (a subsidiary of the Coal Co.). Shareholders in the Coal Company were given first preference to purchase the £10 shares and a dividend of 5% was assured. The whole project proved to be extremely profitable for the shareholders. The Building Company was able to secure government loans of up to half to cost of the building programme at low interest rates "...and the rents actually paid by the Coal Company were sufficient to pay not only five percent dividends, but to permit a sinking fund to redeem the whole capital at the conclusion of the lease, to pay the interest and repayment of Governement loans which were acquired, and to permit heavy depreciation of the houses. The original cost of the houses appears on the books as £59,893 but by 1913 their depreciated value was £4,262." (Michael Cotterill: Mining Museum Research Paper No. 1).

The Lothian Coal Co. leased the houses from the Building Co. for fifteen years from the date of completion and then were able to buy the houses at a fraction of the actual value. The Newbattle and Whitehill Building Co. built no more houses after 1904 but was not wound up until 1914 to ensure the maximum financial benefits could be reaped.

Meantime, another company, the Newtongrange and Easthouses Building Co, had been formed in 1906. It operated in the same way as the previous company erecting houses for the Lothian Coal Co. It was wound up in 1930.

There were three separate districts in Newtongrange at the turn of the century. The old village of Newtongrange now came under the name of Abbeyland and there were the two new schemes of Deanpark and Monkswood. There were no street names (apart from the Loan in Abbeyland) and all the houses were numbered in succession. Deanpark is still like that but Monkswood was changed in 1912 when plans were laid to extend housebuilding as far as the colliery railway line to Easthouses. Part of Monkswood was re-named St. Davids, one street was called Lingerwood Road and the other six streets were named First to Sixth Street. Some larger houses for colliery foremen were built around a large grassed area in 1914. This was called The Square.

Newton Grange Lothian Brass Band, 1905.

Newton Grange quoiters ('kiters').

Andrew Darling with his daughter, 56 St Davids, Newtongrange.

The Weighand family at Stable Row, Newtongrange.

Class at Newbattle School, 1910.

Abbeyland picnic.

The Lockhart family.

The Reid family about 1916. Back row (L to R): Tom, Willie, Davie, Alex. Front row: David, Elizabeth, Annie, Jim.

50

Chapter 7

Village Life: 1900-1920

Some of the families coming in to work for the Lothian Coal Co. at Newtongrange came from other Lothian pits, some came from South Yorkshire (Higginson is a fairly common name in the village) and many came from the West of Scotland. Significant amongst this last group was a large number of Lithuamians or 'Poles' as they were called. Lithuamia had been under Polish role for centuries but was under the rule of Csarist Russia in the 1890s when Lithuanians first began arriving in Scotland. Many were escaping from conscription or persecution by the Russians. Some were actively recruited by Lanarkshire ironmasters to work in the pits and a sizeable community grew up in Bellshill. By 1906 there were about 200 Lithuanians in Newtongrange. In the West of Scotland, it appears the Lithuanians were regarded with suspicion and hostility, but they were popular in Newtongrange and were generally very well treated. The one thing the Lithuanians hated was to be called Poles - it was as bad as calling a Scotsman an Englishmen.

The Lithuanian names caused some difficulty at the pit. Some were given any Scottish name (Joe Sunelaitis became Joe Campbell), some got a name that was similar to their own (the Maliejus family was called Molloy) and some families kept their Lithuanian name (e.g. Dubickas). They were free, of course, to revert to their original name if they had chosen but mostly they were content with their new identity.

The Lithuanians were quiet hard-working, law-abiding citizens but some were notably violent after a heavy drinking bout. Jim Barton remembers, "Albert the Pole was a muckle big strong man. My granny wis a wee wummin and she could quieten him like a moose. If they were drunk at the pub he used tae take a stab oot o' yin o' the gairdens and he would wowf them a'. We wis just wee, ye ken, at the time. My granny came oot, "Pit it doon, Albert." and he pit it doon and lifted her up and walked intae the hoose and put her on a chair and geen her a clap and went away."

These are some of the commonest surnames in Newtongrange - Holgate, Cornwall, Reid, Thomson, Walkinshaw, Moffat, Purves, Duncan, Peacock, McIntosh, Lockhart, Allan, Wilson, Neilson and

Bryson. Nicknames used to be popular amongst the men, though they're not so common now. There was Bander Bob, Band Broon, Oomp McLead and Tommy Blaw, who were all bandsmen. There was Scrappie Gray, Scoop Crichton (a reporter), Trekkle Moffat and Chip per Young who had a chip van that was always parked at Mansfield Avenue (and it was called Chipper Avenue). There was Sweerie Tam, Cleeckie Walkinshaw (who had no hands), Rob Roy (Rob King, the farmer, who was in the drama club and played that part once), Star Blue and Beer or no Beer. Some were not complimentary, like Chimpy, Tattie and the Pups. Certain nicknames run in families. The Reids are usually called Kim and a branch of the Moffats are always called Dobie. In one family there were two brothers called Dobie (Auld Dobie and Young Dobie) and their father was Faither Dobie.

Up until 1902 the only shops in Newtongrange were on John Roman's property. In the Loan there was a grocer, a chemist, a draper, a tailor, a shoemaker and a baker with another grocer in Newbattle Road. Numerous vans served the village. There were milk carts, fish carts and 'soor dook' carts. There were pedlars, fish wives and rag and bone men. The Co-op vans from Gorebridge, Dalkeith and Tranent did especially good business at the beginning of the century. Sandy Fairlie* writes "The trade in Newtongrange had by this time reached large proportions with a van service three times a week. Indeed, on what was known as the 'Pay Saturday', Geordie Smith was in the village the whole day starting off with grocery orders. Most of the customers paid their books to him and so saved themselves the trouble of travelling up to he Central to do so. A lorry followed up with potato and beer orders. This completed, an order of bread was then served to the customers and so quite a busy day for the vanman was completed. It might also be stated that the premises were open on Pay Fridays and Saturdays until 10 p.m."

There was a need for more shops in the village and two plots of land one at each end of the village were reserved by the Coal Co. for feuing to shopkeepers. The one at the bottom end of Newtongrange was first to be taken up. Johnston Armistead built a shop there in 1902. He was a boot and shoemaker who had had a shop for many years on the Loan. His new shop was also the post office. His daughter looked after the shop and post office and Mr. Armitstead had a wee hut at the back where

*Early Coal Mining in Arniston and Newbattle.

he mended shoes. Tom Stewart was another local tradesman who feued a plot to build his own shop. He had had the licensed grocer's at Hope House but he never sought a licence for his new premises next to the Dean.

Willie Reid built a block of six shops in 1906 in Station Road and ran one of them himself as Reid's Beehive Stores. Close by, the Gorebridge Co-op opened extensive new premises in 1908. Their five shops included a grocery, a bakery, a furniture shop, a drapery and a butcher. Round the back were workshops for tailors and bootmakers, delivery van sheds and stables. The Dalkeith Co-op built shops in Station Road before the War. In the 1920s the Dalkeith Co-op was taken over by the Musselburgh and Fisherrow Co-op. Other tradesmen moved into the Loan. Burgari Quinto opened his first shop there in 1905. Jim Barton remembers, "Quinto had a chip shop up the Loan. Ye jist went in. It wis jist a wee room an' a lobby. Ye went in yin at a time an' ye got yer fish supper. Then at the other side o' the pend he hud an ice-cream shop. They hud a billiards hall at the back. Thats where the Poles held their weddin's. It went on for a week. They jist got drunk and sobered up an' startit again."

In 1908 Newtongrange got its first railway station. A *Dalkeith Advertiser* reporter wrote, "During the last dozen years at least the question of providing proper railway facilities has been mooted again and again. The Dalhousie railway station, which since the days of the horse railway has served the population of Newbattle parish, is now closed, and while some slight inconvenience which the people of Newtongrange are now afforded. The fare from Eskbank to Newtongrange in now 1½d. third class (as compared with 1d. formerly to Dalhousie) the distance to the new station being three quarters of a mile longer to the old. The fares to Edinburgh have not been altered, and from Newtongrange to Gorebridge the charge is 2½d. Mr. Thomas Balmer, formerly of Gretna, who recently took up duty at Dalhousie, has been transferred to the new station." (*Dalkeith Advertiser*, 6 September 1908).

People seldom travelled far from their own village in those days and Newtongrange folk were no exception. The Trades Holidays lasted a week but were unpaid and,as no one could afford to go away, a day's excursion to Portobello beach by train was the most anyone could expect. Traditionally, visits to friends outwith he village were made at

New Year, and on the Saturday after Play Day.

All the organisations had an annual excursion by train, bus or farmer's cart to destinations near and far. In 1913 the Gorebridge Co-op trip was to Oban, the Burns Club took 400 to Melrose and the United Free Church chartered a special train to Penicuik for 350 trippers. The Easthouses Sunday School went to Heriot, the Camper's Club reached Peebles in two 'four in hand brakes,' the Baptist Church travelled to Habbies Howe and the Church of Christ Bible Class went to Gullane. Every trip took a musician or two, or even the silver band, to entertain the happy travellers who raced, danced, played and picnicked as long as they were able.

Back home, a popular entertainment for men was provided at regular Sunday afternoon concerts organised by the P.S.A. Brotherhood in the Lothian Halls, P.S.A. stood for 'Pleasant Sunday Afternoon.' This is the report in the _Dalkeith Advertiser_ of one meeting. "The president, Mr. Walkie, presided over a good attendance on Sunday afternoon when Mr. Moffat's orchestra as usual opened the proceedings with spirited selections. The Rev. Robert Ballantyne, M.A. Peebles, in the course of a straight talk to the men as man to man, pointed out the sure evil consequences that would ensure to anyone indulging in strong drink. He urged upon his hearers the value and importance of total abstinence. Mr. Welsh, Musselburgh, rendered two sacred solos with an expression and power that evoked the heartiest appreciation of his hearers. Rev. A. Hardie read the lesson and conducted the devotions, while the President thanked speaker and singers in the name of the meeting." After the picture house opened in 1915 the P.S.A. meetings were held there for many years.

A big occasion in 1913 was the first annual Children's Gala Day. Eighteen hundred children in their best clothes assembled in the public park before marching in procession proudly round the village, led by the Lothian Silver Band. Prizes were awarded to the children carrying the best floral bouquets. The procession finished up at Victoria Park where the children enjoyed sports and refreshments.

A lot of miners enlisted during the First World War. the Durham Light Infantry took over the Lothian Halls and the Band Hall was also commandeered. Many people worked to raise money for the war effort. There was the Our Heroes Fund for Newbattle Parish, a P.O.W. Fund, the National Relief Fund, the Red Cross and there were Christmas War Parcels to be sent to every local man on active service. At home, the Newtongrange Volunteers were organised by Mungo MacKay.

Chapter 8

The Original Dean

The premises occupied by the Dean Tavern were numbered 1,2 and 3 Dean Park, three recently-built terraced houses. No 1 was the manager's house. Nos. 2 and 3 had been converted into a public house by the Lothian Coal Co. at a cost of £400 and furnishing it cost another £147. The Committee paid the normal rent for each house (7/- a week) and were charged 5% interest on the reconstruction costs until the final repayment was made to the Coal Co. directors in 1908, Mrs. Preston remembers, "It wis like an auld-fashioned shop wi' windaes either side. It wis richt auld-fashioned."

The public bar took up most of the ground floor. The bar counter was against one wall and the place was heated with a coal fire. The jug bar was at the side of the building and had its own door. Upstairs was temperance bar where tea, coffee and Bovril were served.

Licensing hours were from eight in the morning until ten at night. Weekends were always the busiest. The men at the pit worked an eleven day fortnight and were paid every second Friday. That was Pay Friday and that night and the following idle day, Pay Saturday, were exceptionally busy.

There were three full time staff - the manager, a barman and a pot boy - with an extra man on at weekends. Andrew Aikman, the manager, had previously worked at the pit but he had lost a leg in an accident and had retired with a pension from the Lothian Coal Co. He got £2 a week, a free house and free coal. Mr. Anderson had sole charge of the till and the clerk, Mr. Gilmour, checked the till at least once a day. Mr. Anderson bought a dog to guard the Dean and was allowed £1 a year for its food. He also had £5 a year towards the expence of hiring a pony.

The second man was paid 21/- a week, increasing gradually to 32/-, and the boy began at 8/- a week increasing to 16/-.

At the first meeting, on October 10th. 1899, the Committee decided to place orders for three grades of whisky from Andrew Usher, a fine quality whisky from Crabbies, bitter ale from Murray of Duddingston, sweet ale and stout from Melvin of Edinburgh, aereated water from Woolleys of Dalkeith and wines, from Andrew Usher. From time to

time, other breweries sought orders from the Dean and Mr. Callender *
made it clear they they would only deal with firms buying coal from
Newbattle Colliery. Small orders for bitter beer were placed with
McEwans and McLennan and Urquart of Dalkeith in 1904. McEwans
beer failed to please and the order was stopped and tit-for-tat,
McEwans stopped their coal order.

There were many complaints relayed to the Committee through Mr.
Pryde and Mr. Taylor, the workmen's representatives, about the quality
of the beer in summertime. The beer was getting too warm and "going
off" so a cold cellar was built in the back garden to remedy this. It was
said that the Abbey Inn served a better pint and Mr. Hood compared a
pint of their beer with a pint of the Dean's but his comments were not
recorded. A request was made by the customers for Younger's beer
instead of Murrays but nothing was done about it.

The Dean Committee closed the Tavern on certain public occasions
and on New Year's Day. It was closed on the day of the funeral of
Queen Victoria and also the on the coronation day of her son, King
Edward VII, in 1902. The village celebrated Coronation Day in the
Public Park and the entertainment included the Lothian Brass Band and
a cycle parade. The Committee decided to close the Dean on the Friday
night before Coronation Day, "as the men might get drunk and not be
fit for work on the Saturday."

More accomodation for drinkers was created in the Dean early on by
erecting a partition upstairs and halving the area of the temperance
room. Drink was sent up on a hoist.

The public bar was draughty and difficult to heat and the Committee
made several attempts to remedy this. The open fire was replaced first
with a stove in 1902 and then with a system of hot water pipes in 1906
and that seemed to be fairly satisfactory. The old bar was taken out that
year and a new horseshoe bar installed. A lot of money was spent in the
first ten years of the Dean trying to improve the place but the premises
were never really suitable for a public house.

The first complete financial year of the Dean's operation (1900-1901)
showed a profit of £340, after paying the court case expenses of £151.
The second year (1901-1902) the total income from the sale of drink was
£3,070 and the profit was £407. Mr. Archibald Hood, chairman of the
*Lothian Coal Co. secretary

Lothian Coal Co., gave a glowing report on the Dean's progress to the thirteenth general meeting of the company on January 27th, 1902. He said that the directors "were considering the advisability of building a concert and lecture hall, recreation and reading rooms and library at Newbattle. A considerable sum of money would be required for this purpose but the directors believed the financial difficulty could be got over by borrowing the money and applying the profits of the Dean Tavern to the payment of the interest and gradual extinction of the debt. Some of the directors had expressed their willingness to advance money for such a good object on the security of the aforesaid profits. They hoped by providing such means of healthy recreation to form counter attractions to those of the public house."(*Dalkeith Advertiser*: 25 September 1902)

Towards the end of 1902, however, sales of alcohol at the Dean Tavern fell and remained fairly poor for three or four years. No further mention was made of a hall until 1907. Various possible reasons for the falling trade were explored by the Committee. The Abbey Inn had a gramophone which was an attraction and some said Mr. Lumsden at the Abbey Inn served a better pint. There was also a bazaar on Mr. Roman's land and that was another attraction. But the main reason was undoubtedly the reduction in pay at the colliery. The daily minimum wage had come down from 8/- in 1900 to 5/9 in October 1902 and then to 5/6 in June 1903. The population of the village was growing rapidly but drink sales remained static. Wage rates remained low until 1907 when they rose to 7/6 a day. Sales at the Dean improved dramatically from £3,000 in 1905-1906 to £5,404 in 1908-1909. Profits more than doubled in those same years from £415 to £992.

It had always been the declared intention of the Lothian Coal Co. to provide a bowling green for Newtongrange from the profits of the Dean and, in the summer of 1900, part of field on the north side of the railway line, near the Dean Oil Works, was obtained from the Marquis of Lothian. The worker's representatives on the Committee wanted the lease to be held by Trustees but the coal company directors decided that the lease should be in the names of the chairman (Mr. A. Hood), the general manager (Mr. J. Hood) and the company secretary (Mr. Callender) and their successors in office.

A greenkeeper, Mr. Rae, was appointed and he was to be given a free house, £1 a week during the season and employment in the pit during the winter. The first year's subscription was set as 5/- and Mr. Callender drafted a set of rules to be approved when there were enough members to hold a meeting. The rules included: no swearing; no gambling; no betting in the pavilion or on the green; and no sales of, or consumption of, alcohol.

The opening ceremony of the bowling green took place on the evening of 29th May 1902. The Lothian Brass Band assembled on the platform roof of the pavilion and played a selection of tunes for 150 invited guests prior to the opening. Hundreds of villagers, mostly men and children, gathered at the entrance to the green to watch the proceedings. Numerous speeches were made by the attending dignatories, including the local ministers, Mr. Carrick and Mr. Hardie, who had both opposed the Dean Tavern licensing application. Mr. Hardie was a total abstainer but Mr. Carrick was not. It is said his horse never passes the Justinless Inn and knew its own way home!

Archibald Hood, chairman of the Coal Co., declared the green open and played the first bowl. "The company were photographed," reported the *Dalkeith Advertiser*, "in front of the pavilion by Mr. Wallace, Dalkeith, and the Committee also had to face the camera. A liberal supply of refreshments (non-alcoholic) were handed round, and what with the band playing and the sun shining the afternoon passed away very enjoyably. The green was well filled with bowlers until dusk." Mr. Hood was presented with a silver jack on a stand as a memento of the occasion.

Most of the profits from the first few years of the Dean Tavern were set aside to pay for the bowling green and it was not until 1904 that the final payment was made. In May 1901, the brass band applied to the Dean for £80 to buy new instruments. The committee offered to contribute £30, Mr. Callender promised £25 on behalf of the Lothian Coal Co. and the band was left to raise the other £25. At the same time, the Committee decided to improve the public park. It was levelled, a base of ashes and redd put down and six inches of topsoil applied. The park was supposed to be for the children but it was only five acres and also contained a cricket pitch. There were complaints that the park was "monopolised" by the cricketers and conversely that the children damaged the pitch. Newtongrange Star, the local junior football team, had their own pitch, Victoria Park, next to the public park.

The Dean Committee paid for a six foot high brick wall around the public park in 1904 and agreed to a seven foot high wall being built around Victoria Park. In fact, only two sides of the wall round the pitch were built at first, owing to a shortage of bricks. The massive house-building programme in the village at this time was the top priority. Between the park and the football pitch ran a path connecting Abbeyland and Monkswood and this got the name Lover's Lane as the high walls created seclusion. Before building the wall the wooden cricket pavilion had to be temporarily removed but in the move it was damaged so the Dean built a new brick pavilion for the cricketers and laid a new pitch for them.

A miniature rifle club was formed in Newtongrange in 1908 and a shooting range, 90 feet long and 9 feet wide, was built alongside the cricket pavilion. "The range is equipped with automatic travelling wire targets, and the firing bench is so constructed as to permit of shooting in the prone, kneeling or standing positions. The targets and firing benches are finely lit by means of the bland incandescent gas burners. The bullets strike on a steel plate at the rear of the range, and immediately drop into a box. It is computed that the cost of fitting and equipping the range will exceed £60 and the money will be furnished out of the profits of the local Gothenburg Public House."* There was also to be an outdoor range at the old quarry at Masterton. *Dalkeith Advertiser: 31st Decem-

On the other side of the cricket pavilion from the rifle range a pigeon house was later built for the Homing Society so they could store their pigeon baskets. The Dean committee also provided a shed for storing quoits at Easthouses and a football pavilion, also at Easthouses, in 1911.

There had been complaints about whippets being trained on the road and on Newbattle Golf Course so the Dean made a track for them in Victoria Park. Whippet racing was a popular sport and races were regularly held in a field at Lingerwood Farm. There was a man who had a dog called 'Beer Or No Beer.' There was beer if it won - no beer if it lost. Thereafter, Newtongrange being a place prone to nicknames, they called the man 'Beer Or No Beer.'

In 1904, the Dean sold 29 gallons of brandy; 224 gallons of rum, gin

*Dalkeith Advertiser: 31st December 1908.

and whisky; 332 barrels of bitter ales; 145 barrels of sweet ales and stouts; 2,656 dozen bottles of bottled ale; 708 dozen bottles of aereated waters; and 102 dozen bottles of wine. Whisky was very cheap in comparison to beer and a lot was drunk, some of it raw spirits as there were no laws about a minimum age for whisky. The government increased the tax on spirits in 1909 and this had an immediate affect on sales. The cheapest whisky sold at the Dean which had previously cost 1/3 a half bottle but was increased to 1/8. After seven months the committee discovered that they had miscalculated the effect of the tax and had been carying too much. The new price was 1/6.

The Committee was seeking other reasons for falling whisky sales at the Dean and were informed that Ballantyne's whisky van from Edinburgh was going round the village and doing good business. Some people thought that Ballantyne's whisky was better than the Dean's and Mr. Taylor was delegated to get a bottle to sample. He brought three bottles of Ballantyne's to the next meeting, priced at 2/6, 3/- and 3/6, according to grade. Mr. Pryde thought the 3/- whisky was the best. The committee then put a little of each whisky in a tin to see how well it would burn. The 3/6 whisky burned the best, but the 2/6 whisky wouldn't burn at all unless mixed with the others. The Dean's cheapest whisky was 3/- (6d. more than Ballantyne's cheapest) and their three other grades were sold at 3/-, 3/6 and 4/-. At the next Committee meeting the members sampled whisky from the Abbey Inn, Rosewell Public House, Ballantyne's cart and the Dean Tavern. The Dean's whisky was thought to be "not so good" as the others and no more was to be ordered from Usher's until they brought it up to their usual standard.

The Committee rebuked the Dalkeith brewers, McLennan and Urquart, on one occasion. It was reported that the brewery was selling barrels of beer "direct to Poles" in the village. The Dean Committee instructed McLennan and Urquart to cease this practice and to only accept orders made directly through the Dean.

Goths were deliberately designed to be austere places in order to discourage drinking, and entertainment of any kind was strictly forbidden. Dominoes were allowed in the Dean at first but they were soon banned as they could be "an inducement for men to enter the public house." The Dean did not give their customers a free drink at New Year, which was the custom in other pubs. It was thought to be "against the spirit of the Dean." Some Committee members wanted to buy a gramophone for the Dean Tavern - the Abbey Inn had one and it was drawing away customers - but the Chief Constable was against the idea.

Though entertainment was forbidden inside the Dean, it was sometimes lively outside. Mrs. Preston remembers, when she was a little girl, seeing people dancing outside the Dean on Pay Fridays, "The band was there and a melodeon, tae. Young yins and auld yins - a' dancin'. Oh, they had a grand time!" This was about 1905. Entertainment of another kind could sometimes be seen on a Saturday night. Boys would gather outside the Dean a little before closing time to see if there were going to be any fights. Jim Reid recalls "Ah've seen quite a few fights, but no' the dirt an muck they fight now. They just had a fair fight. No religion, Orangemen against Catholics, or the like. Ah had an uncle about six feet tall an' he felled a few in his time." Thing's could get out of hand, though. Two men were arrested in the park in 1914 whilst "engaged in a most savage fight surrounded by 100 spectators" (*Dalkeith Advertiser*). They were each fined 7/6 or five days in jail.

The 'Dean Corner' was the regular village meeting place and the Independent Labour Party met there on Tuesday evenings. It is certain that no hall belonging to the Lothian Coal Co. would have been made available to them. Sandy Gardiner, a popular figure in the village, was chairman. He had been quite friendly with Mungo Mackay, the pit manager, until he started up a branch of the Independent Labour Party in Newtongrange but Mr. MacKay fell out with him over that.

A regular and exciting event in the mining villages of the district was the arrival of the travelling gaff or theatre. In a temporary building of canvas and wood, popular plays were performed to enthusiastic audiences. In 1909 a Mr. Snape had put up his gaff behind the Abbey Inn on land belonging to Mr. Romans. Mr. Snape had been going around the Newtongrange shopkeepers seeking prizes for a poetry competition as publicity for his gaff. Word had to to Rev. Hardie, the Free Church minister, that the Dean Tavern, in association with the gaff, was giving away bottles of whisky for a poem written about the Dean. He wrote to the committee demanding an explanation. John Hood, the manager was sent for and explained that he had offered to give Mr. Snape 2/6 as a prize from his own pocket. He was instructed to withdraw his offer and that was that.

Rev. Hardie had been a firm opponent of the granting of the Dean licence in the first place. He had once before written to the committee as he had seen a drunk being ejected from the Dean as he passed one day. There were other problems with drunks. The man who was employed on Pay Fridays to keep out drunks was injured one night, having been attacked by a drunk. He was off his work for more than a week and the Dean paid him 35/6 to compensate for his lost wages. But that kind of incident doesn't seem to have been common.

Each year the Dean got a special licence to sell drink at the Easthouses Games. These were professional games with cash prizes for athletic events, cycle races, whippet racing, quoiting and five-a-side football. Crowds of two or three thousand attended these games. In 1908 the Dean's takings at the Easthouses Games were £53 - 5/- and the Committee gave a donation of £6 to the games committee plus an extra £1 for cleaning up the corks, broken glass, etc. left lying about on the field. The Newtongrange Games were on similar lines and were organised as a fundraising venture by the Brass Band Committee. The Easthouses Games continued until 1915 and were revived briefly in 1931 as amateur games. The Newtongrange Games finished up in 1914 and were never resumed after the war.

What with the rapidly increasing population of the village and relatively high wages, especially in 1907, business at the Dean flourished. The committee discussed an extension to the premises in May 1909 and Mr. Hood agreed to get plans drawn up. The following extract is from the minutes of 21st. September 1909. "The question of increased accommodation in connection with the Dean Tavern was taken into consideration and the chairman stated that Mr. Callender and he had considered this matter very carefully and had come to the conclusion that the present building, which had been altered before to meet the requirements of the increased population could not be satisfactorily altered again and that it would be better to erect an entirely new one. He proposed that a new building be put up immediately behind the present one and that when the new one was ready the present one should be taken down and the ground occupied by it made into an open space or shrubbery before the new building."

Plans for the new Dean had already been drawn up in anticipation of the committee's approval and the architect, Mr. Hardie, was present to explain them in detail. The plans were subsequently passed by the Licensing Board, estimates were sought and were laid before the committee in March 1910. The main contracts went to builders William Black (£937), joiners, Steven and Stoddart (£556) and plumbers, William Thorburn (£470).

Unknown man in front of the original Dean Tavern.

Dean Tavern.

Minute of meeting of committee held in Newbattle Colliery office on Tuesday the 10th day of October 1899 at 6. P.M.

Present.

Mr John Callender in the Chair
Mr m. MacKay
Mr James Baylor
Mr Wm. Pryde Sr.

As the premises in Deanpark Newton-Grange were reported to be nearly ready, it was resolved to commence business on as early a date as possible.

Samples of Beers Spirits &c were submitted and it was resolved to purchase three qualities of whiskey from Andrew Usher & Co. also wines &c from the same firm and one quality fine Whiskey from Crabbie & Co. Leith. Bitter ale from Murray & Co. Duddingston & sweet ale & stout from Metvin & Co. Edinburgh. Aerated waters from Usher & Co. Dalkeith. John Gilmour was appointed Clerk for the Dean Tavern at a Salary of £12. per annum.

This was all the business.

John Callender

The first page of the Dean Tavern Committee Book, dated 10th. October 1899.

Guests at the opening of the Bowling Green (1902). Back row (L to R): Dr. Easterbrook, ?, ?, Rev. A. Hardie (Free Church), ?, John Callender (Lothian Coal Co. secy.) Archibald Hood (managing director), Rev. J. C. Carrick (Church of Scotland), David Carson (behind Mr. Carrick), ?, Frankie Deans, ?, Dr. Inch, ?, Mr. Spark (Inspector of Poor). Front row: Johnnie Gilmour (Dean Tavern Committee secy.) A. Murray Hardie (architect of the Dean Tavern).

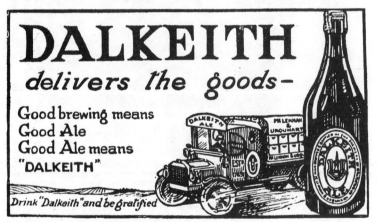
1930's Adverts for Dalkeith Ales.

Chapter 9

The New Dean

No reference was made to the new premises in the Dean Committee minute book between 8 March 1910, when the estimates were accepted, and 28 April 1911, when the annual accounts were presented final costs detailed. There is a single reference in the *Dalkeith Advertiser* of June 2nd 1910, "Though the work of erecting the new "Gothenburg" on a site to the rear of the Dean Tavern is proceeding apace it is expected the premises will not be ready for about four months yet." We must presume the new Dean opened at the beginning of October 1910. There are two reasons for this lack of information. One is that the officials of the Lothian Coal Co. (Mr. Callender, company secretary, and Mr. Mac-Kay, general manager) supervised the work and took all necessary decisions without reference to the committee. The other reason is that the committee was determined not to advertise the Dean directly as that might be seen to be enncouraging drinking, although they were happy to see any project funded by the Dean receive maximum publicity and did not mind the Dean being referred to then.

The Committee had accumulated £3,500 by 1911 and were able to pay all the bills for the building of the new Dean without borrowing. It cost £3,000 plus £600 paid to the Whitehill and Newbattle Building Co. for their three houses (the old Dean) which were demolished.

The new public bar was large and spacious with a horseshoe bar. Three arched pillars supported the roof in the centre of the room. Controversy has often raged in the Dean about the distance from the back wall to the centre of the pillars. It is claimed that it is 24 feet, the same width as goal posts, but there are arguments yet about that. Upstairs, there was a temperance bar, which had its own separate entrance. The other downstairs rooms included a jug bar, a committee room and a private room for meetings and small functions. The main door into the public bar was at the far end from the temperance door, which looked as if it was the main entrance. There was a side door into the bar from Dean Park but it was never much used. All the downstairs walls in the new Dean were tiled with green glazed tiles up to about eight feet from the ground.

One of the earliest functions held in the private room was the Newtongrange Shopkeeper's Dance on March 30th 1911. A company of 40 enjoyed a tea dance with games until the early hours.

This table shows the turnover of the Dean Tavern from 1910 to 1920.

Year	Turnover	Turnover increase or Decrease	Profit
1909-1910	£5,370	-£30	£1,390
1910-1911	£5,410	+£40	£1,240
1911-1912	£5,510	+£100	£1,580
1912-1913	£6,360	+£850	£1,640
1913-1914	£7,950	+£1590	£2,780
1914-1915	£7,390	-£560	£1,990
1915-1916	£5,840	-£1550	£970
1916-1917	£7,080	+£1240	£2,020
1917-1918	£7,330	+£250	£2,230
1918-1919	£8,810	+£1480	£3,040
1919-1920	£12,760	+£3950	£1,300

In 1912 the Lothian Coal Co. began paying the the miner's wages weekly rather than fortnightly and this led at once to an increased turnover. "...weekly pays seem to be making the men spend more on drink." (Dean Minute Book) Higher wages were responsible for the increase in 1913-1914.

During the early years of the First World War the Government became concerned about the effect heavy drinking might be having in the main industrial areas, and licensing hours were controlled under the Defence of the Realm Act in 1915. Pubs had been allowed open all day between 8 am. and 10 pm. until 1914, when the opening time allowed was put forward to 10 am. After 1915 the permitted licensing hours in central Scotland and some other places were reduced to five each day. The Dean Tavern henceforth opened only from 12 a.m. to 2 p.m. and from 6 p.m. to 9 p.m. in the evening for sales of alcohol. This obviously affected sales (as it was meant to) and so did the heavy taxes the Government was imposing on beer and spirits during the war. However, the Dean remained open outside these hours for the sale of non-alcoholic drinks (tea, coffee and Bovril) in the upstairs temperance department.

The largest increase in turnover in the Dean's history occured in 1919-20 due to the exceptionally high wages the men were taking home in that year (15/- a shift minimum - compared to 7/- in 1914).

There was a change in the type of draught beer sold in the Dean in 1916. Strong beer had long been popular but due to greatly increased wartime liquour duties and higher raw material costs the price of a pint had risen to 8d. Beer bought at the jug bar was the same price but half the strength and so double the quantity was supplied. In the summer of 1916 two sample barrels of light ale were ordered to see how they would go. At 6d. a pint, light beer was immediately popular and sales of heavy beer dwindled to such an extent that no more was ordered. Whisky and rum cost 8d. or 9d. (10d. for special) a gill. A nip was half a gill. By 1918 beer of all kinds was in short supply and individual publicans had their own systems of rationing. Jim Barton remembers, "There were no treatin' durin' the First War. Ah couldnae take you a pint and yon couldnae take me a pint – individual only. Ye daurnae gaun intae company wi geein' each other drink."

Working hours for the bar staff were long. The waiters started at 9 a.m. and spent the morning clearing up, washing bottles and bottling beer. They were allowed a break from 4 p.m. - 6 p.m. "if work permitted" and finished at 10 p.m. From 9 p.m. to 10 p.m. only the temperance bar was open but, in October 1915, the committee decided to close the temperance bar outside licensing hours, as the takings were only 1/- a day at most. This meant the staff could get home an hour earlier.

For the first few years of the Dean the staff changed very little. Only two employees left in the first twelve years but by 1911 it was becoming difficult to find and keep a good pot boy because of the long hours. An advert in The Scotsman and the Evening Dispatch in October 1915 brought only two replies. One boy was invited for an interview but he never turned up. Similar difficulties were found in the Committee's efforts to employ a third barman in 1912. The first man engaged stayed only a week and five others were employed in the next two years for varying periods. The wages were 28/- a week.

The waiters were expected to look smart. Jim Barton: "Ye hud yer long white apron on. We bocht oor ain aprons, tain them hame an washed them. Ye hud tae wear a collar an' tie." No smoking or drinking was allowed on duty. An anonymous letter writer once accused the waiters of smoking at work and this led to a severe warning by the Committee.

On December 31st. 1915 the manager of the Dean Tavern, John Hood, was tragically knocked down by a bus near the police station and died as a result of his injuries. He had worked at the Dean since it opened in 1899, beginning as pot boy. He became second man in 1904 and was promoted to manager at the age of 22 on the death of Andrew Anderson in 1907. Mrs, Hood was given two weeks wages (£5) and £150 by the Committee and was allowed the remain in her house for six months. It was suggested she might get £1 a week until she had recovered her health and was able to work. The balance could then be invested for her or used for business.

John Purves, who had been second man since 1908, was appointed as manager in John Hood's place.

The directors of the Lothian Coal Co. had planned, since the opening of the bowling green in 1902, to build a hall, recreation rooms, reading room and library in Newtongrange but sagging profits at the Dean Tavern had delayed the project until 1910. By then profits from the Dean were well over £1,000 a year and still rising. Despite being committed to the expense of building a new public house the Dean Committee decided to go ahead with plans for an Institute but on a reduced scale. It had been estimated that £5,000 - £6,000 would be needed to build a hall with recreation rooms, etc. This was too much, so the hall was cut out, thus halving the cost. The money was to be borrowed from the Lothian Coal Co. at 5% interest and repaid when the new Dean Tavern was paid for. The Committee was expending a lot of money at this time on the basis of future profits, which could not be guaranteed. It was made clear that no committee member could be responsible for any debt incurred. The Dean sales in fact dropped back a bit in 1910, as wages had dropped to 30% below those of 1907. Nevertheless, the Dean Committee continued with its programme of building, erecting a football pavilion at Easthouses and a Band Hall at Newtongrange both in 1911.

The Institute was ceremoniously opened on the Saturday afternoon of April 20th 1911 by James Hood, managing director of the Lothian Coal Co. The silver band played through the streets beforehand and 500 of the Newtongrange residents turned up to watch the proceedings. The

Dalkeith Advertiser began a long and admiring report thus - "Of the many benefits conferred on the community of Newtongrange from the profits accruing from the Dean Tavern, the local public house conducted on the Gothenburg principle, none will probably be more appreciated than the Newbattle Institute."

The Institute was brick-built and harled, with red sandstone dressings. It was described as being in the 'English renaissance' style and stood on the Main Street in the Dean Park district of the village. Inside there was included a billiard room with three tables. Round three sides of this room there was a raised platform with settees on it and there was room for other games in an adjoining alcove. The reading room had eight long tables with racks of newspapers along one wall. There were shelves to hold a thousand books for the lending library and small tables for games or reading. Other facilities included a temperance refreshment room, a kitchen and lavatories. There was also a house for the caretaker, Mr. Kinnaird.

Mr. Hood, in his opening speech, acknowledged that other mining villages had built Institutes before they had in Newtongrange but he thought their facilities were unsurpassed. Membership was 1d. a fortnight and he hoped everyone would join. The Institute was to be managed by a committee of ten - five officials of the Coal Company (including the manager director, the Chairman and the secretary) and five workmen elected at a public meeting.

The Institute was very popular and there was great demand for use of the billiard tables, especially. The reading room was well used but it proved impossible to play dominoes quietly and avoid aggravating the readers. In March 1914 an extension to the Institute was opened with ample space for billiards, a separate games room (giving peace in the reading room), a smoking room. The cost was £2,500 and it was borrowed as usual from the directors of the Lothian Coal Company.

Mr. Hood was chairman of the Dean Committee until 1917 but when he was absent from meetings (as he was frequently) his place was taken by Mr. Callender, the Coal Co. secretary. Indeed, Mr. Callender took many of the decisions concerning the Dean Tavern. He continued on the Committee for six years after his retiral as secretary. He spent much of his spare time working for the good of the community and he was well liked locally. He was honorary president of the P.S.A. and vice president of the Miniature Rifle Club, a J.P., County Councillor for Newbattle Parish Council for 20 years and a member of Newbattle School Board for 22 years. Mr. Callender retired from the Dean Committee in 1917. His place was taken by James Murray, his successor as company secretary. The chairman from that time on was Mungo MacKay, general manager at the pit and a man who wielded a great deal of influence in Newtongrange.

The Dean Committee undertook another large scale project before the First World War. There had been a picture house in Newtongrange since about 1912. It was on a piece of waste ground at the back of the last row of houses at Abbeyland, opposite Coo Mary's house. 'Evans's' Picture Palace was a temporary sort of building with wooden walls and a canvas roof. The projection box stuck out the back to ensure "absolute safety for the public". There was a complete change of programme every night with two shows on Saturdays - prices were 6d. 4d and 3d to sit on wooden benches. The children's matinee on Saturday afternoons cost 1d or 2d but a jeely jar got you in to the 1d seats and if you couldn't even scrounge a jeely jar you could "skin in" sometimes.

Word got to the Dean Committee early in 1913 that "some persons had applied for ground for a picture house in the village." They considered whether to build a picture house themselves so they could have some control over the pictures shown and agreed to do so if there was no competition. Meanwhile, plans were going ahead to build a picture house on ground belonging to Mr. Romans behind the Abbey Inn where the shows were held. Mr. Walker, tenant of the Abbey Inn, was behind the scheme but it foundered and the Dean went ahead with their own plans. The Dean Committee didn't want to run the picture house themselves and advertised for tenants before it was built. The applicants were Mr. Herman of Dalkeith Picture Palace; Mr. Wilson, who had a cinema in the Forrester's Hall, Dalkeith, Mr. Evans of Newtongrange Picture Palace and the Burntisland Picture Palace Company, whose offer of £325 a year was accepted.

The site that was chosen by Mr. Hood and Mr. Callender was at the top of the village opposite the Dean Oil Works. Three shops were to be incorporated into the building scheme, the first shops at the top end of Newtongrange.

The estimated price for the picture house, in May 1914, was £6,000 and the building was finished by the end of the year. John Lockart remembers the picture house being built when he was six or seven years old. Before that it was just a field "wi' a muckle big tree richt on the corner."

The *Dalkeith Advertiser* of December 17th 1914 carried the first advertisement for the Newtongrange Picture Palace with the words "Look out for opening announcement next week!" and asked for applications for the following jobs - general manager, cash girl check girls (2) and men checkers (2). There was no announcement on December 24th nor on December 31st but this notice appeared on January 7th 1915. "Newtongrange Picture Palace, nightly at 7.30 pm, Saturdays 7.00 pm and 9.00 pm, four changes of programme weekly, admission 3d, 4d, 6d and 9d, matinees Saturday at 3.00 pm admission 1d." The first film to be shown was 'Out of the Depths' on Thursday and Friday, changing to 'Cinderella' on Saturday. Patrons were promised "drama, interest, latest war pictures, comic and Keystone comedies."

The final cost of building the Picture Palace was £6,440 and £5,000 was borrowed from the Lothian Coal Co. directors. The committee members, as before, emphasised that they were not personally responsible for the cost of the picture house and that the Lothian Coal Co. would have to bear the cost if the profits of the Dean were not maintained. Fortunately the profits were substantial and the full cost of the Picture Palace was paid up by the Committee in 1918, just three years after it was built.

One of the shops in the picture house building was let to a watchmaker, Andrew McGowan, one to a barber, Aubrey Hirst, and the third, on the corner of Main Street and Murderdean Road, was let to William Scott, ex-manager of the Dean Oil Works, as a fruit and confectionery shop.

The Dean Tavern (built 1910) with Andrew Aikman, manager, (centre) and Tom Reid, barman, (right). The old Dean stood in the open space at the front.

Inside the Dean, 1925. Behind the bar (L to R): Bob McKinlay, Tom Hackett (manager), Andrew Aikman. Customers: 2nd from right, Mr. Preston; 3rd from right, Sandy Peatie.

Newtongrange Picture Palace (opened 1915).

Newbattle Institute, Newtongrange (opened 1911).

The Institute reading room.

The Institute billiard room.

THE PALACE, Newtongrange.

PHONE————————GOREBRIDGE 63.

Thursday, Friday, Saturday,
This Week.

One House on THURS. and FRIDAY at 6 30.

Two Houses on SATURDAY at 6.15 and 8 45.

Matinee on Sat. at 3.   Ad. 2d.

Penitentiary.

(A) WITH

WALTER CONNOLLY,

Joan Parker, John Howard, Robert Barrat.

Drama whipping your Emotions to Fever Pitch! Love in the "big house"! Murder in the Cell Blocks! Terror in the Horror "Hole"! Rooking the Screen with Fury!

Dodge City Trail.

(U) FEATURING

Charles Starrett and Donald Grayson.

Outdoor Villiany. Lively Western, Blended with Song.

Monday, Tuesday, Wednesday,

Next Week.

2 Houses on Monday at 6.15 and 8 45.

1 House on Tuesday and Wednesday at 6 30.

MANHATTAN MELODRAMA

(A) STARRING

CLARK GABLE,

MYRNA LOY,

WILLIAM POWELL,

Nat Pendleton, Isabel Jewell, Leo Carrillo, and Mickey Rooney.

Powerful Triangle Melodrama.

Sensational Acting and Tense Dramatic Atmosphere.

COMEDIES, NEWS, Etc.

Next Week-End—Duggie Wakefield and his Gang, "CALLING ALL CROOKS."

PRICES—6d, 9d, 1s. Children, 4d, 5d, 6d (Full Price Saturdays)

1930 advertisement from the Dalkeith Advertiser.

Chapter 10

The Bottom Shop

The Abbey Inn has long been known locally as the 'Bottom Shop.' In the old days a pub was also a shop and the term is still used by the licensing trade. It first got a public house licence in 1897 when Alexander Henderson was the licensee. Charles Lumsden took over in 1900 and he had it until 1909 when John Romans let it to William Walker. Mr. Walker, however, had a little difficulty getting the licence transferred to his name. William Stark, janitor at Newbattle School, and Rob King, farmer, objected at the Licensing Court meeting and tried to get the licence withdrawn. A letter had been delivered to 800 householders in Newtongrange and the surrounding district by the temperance societies. The following is a copy of the letter.

NEWTONGRANGE
30th March, 1909.

Dear Sir or Madam,

As it is now generally recognised that the question of the continuance or non-continuance of licenses to sell drink in any locality is a question that should be settled by the voice of the people; we, the undersigned, respectfully invite the householders of Newtongrange and surrounding districts, in view of the forthcoming licensing courts to take advantage of the enclosed form to indicate their mind on the above question so that the licensing Magistrate may be assisted and guided in the with-holding and granting of licenses

(Rev.) ALEXANDER HARDIE. President of Newbattle U.F. Total Abstinence Society.
JAMES TAYLOR. President of Newbattle Band of Hope.
GEORGE PHILIP Chief Ruler of the Rechabites, Newtongrange
ALEX. LECKIE Chief Templar of "Guiding Star" Lodge, Newtongrange
GEORGE WOOD Right Worshipful Patriarch, Sons of Temperance, Newtongrange.

N.B. To be called for in a day or two. Please fill up and sign.

THE BOTTOM SHOP

VOTING FORM

1 Prohibitory Resolution(means that no certificate for the sale of excisable liquors shall be granted).

2 Limiting Resolution(means that the number of certificates for sale of excisable liquors shall be reduced).

3 No Change Resolution(means that the existing conditions shall continue)

Please indicate your vote by making a X in the right hand space opposite the Resolution for which you vote.

Signature of the Householders. ....

The results of the poll were read out at the Licensing Court meeting. 299 forms were returned signed and properly filled up and of these 81 voted for no change in the licenses, 44 voted for limited licences and 174 voted for total prohibition. Counsel for the objectors claimed that this was "an overwhelming majority" in favour of prohibition. This was not accepted by the court, nor did the court think that two public houses was too many for a population of 5,000 "almost entirely composed of members of the mining trade." Mr. Walker was granted his licence unanimously.

There was a letter from an anonymous correspondent in the Dalkeith Advertiser during the course of the licensing controversy, demanding to know the turnover of the Dean. Part of the letter read, "The conscience of the community has been debauched by the bribes and doles distributed by the "Reformed" Public House establishment in the place."

In 1910 there was a fight in the Abbey Inn between a waiter and two East Calder miners over the price of a dozen bottles of beer. During the disturbance the waiter got a black eye. Two days later the two miners were seen passing the Abbey Inn going towards Newbattle. Mr. Lumsden and the waiter followed the men down the Peth and gave then a hammering. Mr. Lumsden was fined £3 and the waiter, John Kerr, £1 for their actions.

Mr. Walker bought the licensed grocer's shop at Hope House on Newbattle Road from John Stout in 1915. You could only have one licence at a time in those days and so Walker put Tom Hackett in the grocer's as manager and licensee. Tom Hackett was Mr. Walker's "guid brother" - they were married to two sisters.

Jim Barton worked in Hackett's as a boy. He remembers, "The beer came in barrels and we bottled it, like o' stout and Bass. We bottled that in the grocer's and we barried it up tae the Bottom Shop. Bass had tae lie about four tae six weeks before ye could really take the cork oot tae let a' the sediment drap tae the bottom, then it wis a' clear. As sin as ye yaised that barrel ye bottled another yin an' pit the bottles at he side o' it - bottled on such and such a day - and by the time ye got that sellt this yin wis ready. It wisnae long in goin'. A lot o' folk drunk Bass then. After that they tried draught Bass but it widnae take and then it yaist tae gaun off in hot weather. Ye had it in the cellar an' ye'd tae keep cold bags on the tap o' it - a gless o' cauld water on it. That wis tae cool it doon or it wid go. When ye did start tae bottle it ye daurny stop. Ah did that when ah wis bottlin' it first - ah didnae ken, of course - an' ah got a slap on the mooth for it. That wis Walker. Tae pit the Bass oot ye'd tae hud the bottle a certain way and watch it fillin' afore the sediment came and then stop. That was yer bottle o' Bass and that was 6d a bottle. Now, Bass is different. Ye can turn Bass oot. There's nae ingredients in it noo."

Jim Barton recalls some of Mr. Walker's business practices: "An' then he got in as much sugar an' he got in a barrel o' treckle an' a barrel o' seerup an' ye had tae take 5/- worth o' messages before ye got a pund o' treckle or seerup or a pund o' sugar."

Jim later went to work in the Bottom Shop under Mr. Walker "He was a great man! He never drunk. He had a bottle o' cold tea on the side an' a traveller came in an' he would say, "Ye'll take a dram, Mr. Walker an' gee the boy a shilling. The shilling went intae the till an' he would take his gless - but his gless o' tea- and cherge him the full price o' it. he never drunk."

The Bottom Shop's opening hours were from 4 pm. to 9 pm. after 1915. Jim Barton remembers. "During the First War I've seen them standing there at half past three, richt up tae the White Gates in a queue waitin' tae get in at fower o' clock. But Walker was richt cute efter that. He went an' got a licence for tae sell drink. Ye could order it an' ah could carry it oot intae the coo park - that's where the Legion is now. They used tae come an' order half a dozen bottles o' beer and a gill o' whisky, ye ken, and I hid tae take it oot.

Walker, he used tae open the door at fower o' clock and on the coonter wis a gless o' whisky an' a pint o' beer, a gless o' whisky and a pint o' beer, repeated richt doon a' the coonter. Ah stood at the door - ah was only a young laddie - and let them in and coonted them. Ah let in so many an they drank their gless o' whisky and their pint o' beer an oot they went an' in came another crowd. By the time they were goin' oot they were fillin' up the glesses again.

There were 54 gallon hoggets* and Walker used tae bottle it - half pint bottles - an' at a certain time at night the beer went off. Only bottled beer left 6d. a bottle. He was makin' 3d off every pint. He had 80 dozen bottles ready. An' he bottled it off o' the fraught beer an' that wis what he din.

A lot o' whisky came in bottles but Walker boucht it in bulk. He reduced it his ainsel'. Six big barrels at the top o' the bar and we pumped it intae the barrels an' it had four wee taps. It was Walker's Special. Ye got it over the proof. Ye reduced it to 70 by addin' water.

Then the tramps used tae come in there wi' their jeely jars for beer. There was a man wi' a dug's collar. He had a big collar right up tae his neck like a minister."

Mr. Walker had bought the Bottom Shop from the trustees of the late John Romans in 1918 and in 1923 he sold it to the Lothian Coal Co, who owned it for the next 25 years. During that time the licencees were the Montgomerys, who owned Woolleys' of Dalkeith, the lemonade manufacturers.

* hogshead

The Loan, Newtongrange, showing the Abbey Inn, Romans's Buildings in the background and one of the Abbeyland houses on the right.

The Dean Tavern staff in 1923. Left to right: Andrew Aikman, James Dickson, Thomas Hackett, James Barton, Robert McKinlay, Robert Haldane and Alex Naysmith.

Miss Baird and her class at Newbattle School.

The organisers of the Soup Kitchen during the 1921 Strike in Newtongrange.

Johnnie Williamson outside his shop in the Loan. He moved to Main Street when the Loan was demolished in the 1930's.

Date	Competition	Venue	Star	Opponent	
1 aug	League	Home.	4	Roswell Rosedale	1
6 "	League	Away.	3	Edinburgh Rosebery	0
9 -	League	Home.	3	Wemyss Athletic	0
13 -	League	Home.	1	West Calder Juniors	1.
15 -	League	Home.	4	Bonnyrigg Rose	3.
20 "	League	Away	3	Penicuik Juniors	0.
24 "	League	Away	0	Edinburgh Emmet	1.
27 "	League	Home.	1	Tranent Juniors	2
31 "	League	Home	5	Arniston Rangers	0.
3 Sept.	League	Away.	1	Loanhead Mayflower	0
10 "	Scottish Cup	Away	2	Penicuik Juniors	0
17 "	Musselburgh Cup	Away.	1	Rosewell Rosedale.	0
24 "	East of Scotland Cup	Away.	0	Penicuik Juniors	1.
1 Oct	Simpson Shield.	Away	2	Dalkeith Thistle	2.

Date	Competition	Venue	Star	Opponent	
1921-22				Star	
18 April	League	Home	4	Leith Amateurs	1
22 "	League	Home	2	Musselburgh Bruntonians	1
25 "	League	Home	1	Loanhead Mayflower	0.
28 "	League	Away	4	Leith Amateurs	1
2 May	League	Home	3	Edinburgh Rosebery	1.
6 "	League	Away	2	Broxburn Athletic	0
17 "	League	Away	3	Bonnyrigg Rose	1.
30 "	Marshall Cup	Away	2	Dalkeith Thistle	0
5 June	Marshall Cup	Home	1	Musselburgh Bruntonians	0
10 "	Marshall Cup	Olive Bank	1	Portobello Thistle	0

1921-22.	Played	Won	Lost	Drawn	Goals For	Agst	Points
League	34	24	5	5	77·	29.	53
Cup-Ties	20	12	5	3.	30	18	
Total	54	36	10	8.	107·	47.	

Pages from a notebook kept by the late John Armstrong with some of Newtongrange Star's results for 1921-22. Mr. Armstrong was a notable village personality. In the early years of the century the weekly football results were displayed in the post office.

Chapter 11

The Period of the Mortar Tub

The combination of a world-wide coal famine and a shortage of labour had pushed coal to an unprecedented £4 a ton in 1920 compared to 13/5 a ton in 1913. Suddenly demand for coal fell dramatically. Foreign buyers, who had previously purchased British Coal, were able to obtain cheaper supplies from America. The Government found they were subsidising the pits at the rate of £2,000,000 a week and hurriedly announced the end of the Coal Emergency Act.

Wage rates had reached 20/6 a shift and the coal owners, when they regained control of the mines, immediately announced a wage reduction. The Miners' Federation refused to accept the decrease and a national strike began on 1st April 1921. The strike lasted three months and the rates at the return to work were 8/5 a shift.

During the strike the unions had called out the safety men and many pits were seriously flooded before the troops took over. Adam Haldane recalls, "We made up oor mind efter the '21 Strike we widnae stop pumpin'. We aye allowed the safety men intae the pit. The Miners' Union decided it was foolish because we'd aye have tae go back."

There was a short-lived boom in the coal trade in 1924, at the end of which the coal owners sought to cut their costs by doing away with the minimum rates, increasing the working day by an hour thus cutting wages drastically. The Government, faced with a crippling strike, decided to subsidise the coal industry for nine months until May 1st 1926 to prevent the wage cut. When the subsidy came to an end on that date, and the miners still refused to accept the employers terms, they were locked out. A general strike was called to support the miners on May 4th but it lasted only nine days. The miners felt they had been be-trayed by the "ignominious surrender"* of the other Trade Union leaders. The emergency Powers Act of 1920 had been put into force on April 30th 1926 and the pits were guarded by troops. At Newtongrange, soldiers with rifles were stationed on the railway bridge (the Coronation Brig) over Murderdean Road. It is said that they had instructions to shoot any miner approaching the pit. The soldiers were billeted in the

* R. Page Arnot, A History of Scottish Miners

pit workshops. Eventually, after seven bitter months, the miners called off the strike and returned to work on the employer's conditions.

There had been no new houses built in Newtongrange for several years after the First World War due to a shortage of men and materials. A huge house building programme was begun by the coal owners of Mid and East Lothian in 1923 and the Lothian Coal Co. was at the forefront of this activity. A.S. Cunningham in his book 'Mining in Mid and East Lothian', published in 1925, refers to this as "the period of the mortar tub." In the three years between 1924 and 1927 a total of 269 houses were built, completing Fifth and Sixth Street and creating five new streets, Seventh Street to Tenth Street and Park Road. Temporary railway tracks were laid up the centre of these streets to give easy access for building materials. "Houses for officials of the colliery are two storeys in height, of four and five apartments; while the cottages for miners are one storey. Features of the houses are bathrooms sculleries and all modern conveniences." (A.S. Cunningham).

In 1925 a primary school was built in Sixth Street next to the new children's play area in the Welfare Park. This relieved the overcrowding in Newbattle Public School, which then became exclusively a secondary school. A school for the Roman Catholic children of Newtongrange and Gorebridge was opened about 1924 at Newtonloan Toll, midway between the two villages.

The joint founder of the Lothian Coal Co., Archibald Hood, was managing director from 1890 until his death in 1902 and managing director between 1900 and 1902. His son, James Hood, took over as managing director in 1902 and then as chairman in 1911. He held both these posts until 1941. Archibald and James Hood were both skilled mining engineers but they had other extensive business interests in Scotland and Wales which kept them away from Newbattle much of the time. For over 40 years the detailed planning and management of the pits and villages belonging to the Lothian Coal Co. was in the hands of Mungo MacKay, the company agent and general manager. His domination over the village of Newtongrange in that time has become legendary.

Mungo MacKay was first employed by the Lothian Coal Co. in 1890 as under manager at Whitehill Colliery. He later moved to Polton and in 1894 was appointed manager at Newbattle at the age of 27. "In conjunction with Mr. James A. Hood, managing director, he was largely responsible for the planning and layout of Newtongrange, which has made it a model mining community, so far as housing and recreational facilities are concerned. In the latter connection the provision of an Institute for the workers of the Newbattle district, the erection of a cinema and the opening of various sports centres were largely due to his initiative and enterprise."(*Dalkeith Advertiser*: 16 March 1939)

Mungo MacKay was a brilliant mining engineer and largely due to his foresight, business acumen, management skills and technical knowledge, the Lady Victoria Pit gained a reputation as a model of innovation and good mining practice. "Always well abreast of the times, Mr. MacKay was responsible for the introduction of new ideas and modern appliances, which gave the pits he managed the reputation of being among the best regulated and equipped in the country."(*Dalkeith Advertiser*: 16 March 1939)

Mungo MacKay lived in an imposing house opposite the Lady Vic, a short way from the Colliery Office. His own office was upstairs and anyone in the village guilty of an offence would be sent for, to go "up the stairs" where Mr. MacKay sat at the famous "green table" with the company policeman standing behind. Tony Campbell remembers "Mungo MacKay was the heid yin in the village. Some folk respected him. The gaffers, they were kinnae scared o' him. Ye hear plenty stories. Ah never had any dealin's wi' him." John and Tom Lockhart: "He was a' right. He wis strict right enough. He was respected tae. Ah dinnae think onybody liked him. When they seen him comin' they yist tae hide." Mrs. Preston: "He wisnae a nice man. He was like Hitler. Folk were feart at losin' their hooses. He came doon on the engine frae Easthooses an' he could look right intae their back kitchens. An' if they wernae kept right they were tellt tae sort them." If a miner failed to keep his garden properly someone was sent in to tidy it up and the cost was deducted from the man's wages.

George Armstrong: "Ah'll gie him his due he wis a guid minin' engineer but he wis a hard man, a hard man. If you done anything wrong at all ye had tae go up afore him up tae what they cried the Green Table an' ye had tae huv a collar an' tie on afore ye seen him an' if he fined ee, it was 10/- donation to the Royal Infirmary. That wis yer fine, 10/- donation to the Royal Infirmary."

You could be sent for for all reasons. Jim Barton was summoned for whistling in the billiard room at the Institute, Steve Moore was sent for (with his dad) when he was 10 years old for riding a pit pony in a field at Lingerwood Farm and Davie Paul was "skylarking" on a roof at the pit. Sometimes you just got a row but fines were common. The standard fine was 10/-but it could be as much as £2 and it was always a donation to the Royal Infirmary. This went on until one time Jack Bradley was fined £2 for smoking underground and he went back to the Infirmary and told them it was a fine. They never accepted a penny after that.

Mungo MacKay always seemed to know what was going on in the village. Tony Campbell: "There was always a spy in the camp. There was always somebody cliped."Jim Barton: "If ye done anythin' wrong spies reported ye tae Mr. MacKay. Ye didnae ken whae the spies wir. Ah could be speaking' tae you an' you could be the spy. Ah wouldnae ken if ah wis tae tell you somethin' an' you wis tae gaun up an' tell MacKay. Ah've nae idea whae it wis."

The colliery officials were expected to interest themselves in village societies and they were usually office bearers in them. "It wisnae class distinction altogether. They knew how to talk and they knew about rules. And, of course, Mungo MacKay got all the information back." (Jim Reid)

Tony Campbell remembers seeing Mr. Hood on his rare visits to Newtongrange. He remembers he was "swell dressed in a fawn, nap coat. He carried a walking stick an' he had a limp. He was with Mr. MacKay and the two of them came in the main gates. Dod Hamilton had a wee hut beside the gates, and he checked the coal cart, as they left. He kept a goose wi' him. Well, this goose got away one day an' it made straight for MacKay and Hood. Mr. Hood kept it away with his stick. We took it for granted that Dod would catch it - but ah never knew actually what happened. I never found out. The goose was around for a while after that."

Mr. MacKay was on the Dean Committee from the beginning in 1899. He was chairman from 1917 until his death in 1939. Jim Barton: "MacKay wis the main man. He came intae committee meetings in the back room. He was never in the bar. They rung the bell when they were feenished if they wanted a drink. MacKay never drunk.

He stopped the foremen drinkin' in the Dean. The blacksmith foreman would sherpen yer picks and dreels an' ye would gie them a bit nip.

MacKay downed it. "Ye'll no' gaun intae the Dean," an' he stopped them gaun intae the Dean. But the contractors came in. They wis aye a'thegither."

Frank Taylor was the Lothian Coal Company policeman. He was a member of the County Constabulary but all his work was tied up with the Coal Company. One of his jobs was to allocate houses to miners in Newtongrange. It is said that the better houses went to the favoured, or those with £2 or £3 to spare.

At Mungo MacKay's funeral, "There were very few people out. It just passed very fleetingly by." (Tony Campbell)

Newtongrange was undoubtedly a well-regulated village in Mr. MacKay's time and his regime has its supporters. Alec Trench: "If Mungo MacKay wis here today this would be a different village. That village wid never be allowed tae go dilapidated the way it is now if Mac-Kay had been here."

The major decisions about the running of the Dean Tavern and the use made of its profits were always made by the Coal Company representatives on the Dean Committee. During the '20s and '30s the Lothian Coal Co. representatives were Mungo MacKay and James Murray, the company secretary. There were two members representing the miners and both served for life. When one died the remaining Committee members decided on a suitable replacement. Mungo MacKay was the decision maker and it is clear that most of the Dean business was determined outwith the Committee meetings. Usually major decisions were at least formally discussed but occasionally there was no discussion. For example in the 1926 Minutes: "Mr. MacKay mentioned that the two cottages being built on the site of the picture house were to be property of this Committee and that we would be charged for the building of the same."

On one occasion Mr. MacKay did not get his own way. In 1936, the Newbattle Welfare Committee had a deficit of £1,350 and Mr. MacKay tried to get the men at the pit to pay an extra penny a week Welfare money. They refused and the Dean Committee agreed to pay the deficit when they had enough money.

In 1920 there was a brief threat to the continuation of the Dean Tavern when a Veto Poll was requested in Newtongrange by local prohibition supporters under the terms of the 1913 Temperance Act to vote on whether the village should become a 'dry' area. In the months preceding the poll there was a 'No Licence' Campaign run by the Citizen's Council and an Anti-Prohibition Campaign. The results of the poll were No Change - 863, Limited Licence - 7, No Licence - 210.

The turnover of the Dean reached a peak of nearly £15,000 in the year 1920-1921 when wages were at a record level but it fell back by a third year after. Profits were generally above £1,500 a year though were a bit lower in the 1930s.

Annual grants of £5 to £10 were given by the Committee to various local organisations such as the Rifle Club, the Flower Show, the Cage Birds Society, the Homing Pigeon Club, the Gala Day and the Ambulance Association. The Bowling Club always had regular support and any repairs or improvements were paid by the Dean. Other organisations receiving accasional help were the Burns Club, the cricket club and the school football and netball teams. The Quoiting Club got £5 a year between 1922 and 1926 when it folded. Quoiting had been a very popular sport in the district in previous days.

Newtongrange Star F.C. had played no matches during the First World War and their pitch and pavilion were badly neglected. They applied to the Dean Committee in 1919 for a grant to help re-start the club. The pavilion needed rebuilding and the gates and fences were broken down. The War Memorial Committee proposed that the old pitch be used as part of an extension to the public park and the Dean Committee decided to provide a new pitch and pavilion for the Star beside the bowling green at Murderdean Road.

The pavilion when it was built in 1923 was, in the words of the *Dalkeith Advertiser* reporter, "a capacious structure, which, in appearance and size, surpasses those belonging to many senior clubs. The Star will be in the proud position of being the first junior club in Midlothian - if not in the whole of Scotland - to possess a grandstand." Besides dressing rooms and showers for both teams and the referee, the grandstand also contained a room with a boxing ring for Newtongrange Boxing Club; a room for the Pigeon Club; one for the Quoiting Club; another for the Miniature Rifle Club (to replace their range in the public park) and another room which was set aside for the Radio Association.

There was a running track round the pitch and a quoiting ground beside the grandstand. It was estimated that the ground would hold 20,000 to 30,000 spectators. The cost of the whole project was £5,000.

There had been plans to build an Institute at Easthouses since 1914 but the war intervened. In 1918 plans were revived but postponed until materials and labour were available. The Easthouses Institute was finally built on similar lines to the one at Newtongrange in 1925. It cost £4,000 and was almost the last building to be erected at the expense of the Dean Tavern. Thereafter, most of the Dean profits were used in maintaining earlier buildings and supporting existing organisation, sometimes to a considerable degree.

The planned extension of the public park was undertaken with money, not from the Dean Tavern profits, but from the funds of the District Miner's Welfare Committee for Mid and East Lothian. One penny was levied on every ton of coal produced in Great Britain and the money was to be spent on recreation, health and education in the mining areas. The park was begun in 1924 and opened on September 11th, 1926. *Dalkeith Advertiser*: 16 September, 1926 "Viscount Chelmsford, who was accompanied by Commander Coote, R.N., formally opened the park, claimed to be the first of its kind in Scotland. It extends to about 17 acres and has a putting green with separate pavilion, and a children's play centre. There is a bandstand in the centre of the park, whilst there are flower-beds and shrubs, and a rockery with numerous herbaceous plants are among the other features. The park has cost about £9,000."

Lord Chelmsford was the chairman of the Central Welfare Committee in London and Commander Coote had designed the children's play centre, which was the first of its type in Scotland.

Preceding the formal opening was a ceremony in the Square Park when Mary Allan; dux girl of Newbattle School, was crowned Queen by Mrs. Fowler, the headmaster's wife.

In 1925 the Dean Committee undertook "to pay the wages of the workmen in the Welfare Park meantime." This was £507 in the first year. Payments continued intil 1950 when Midlothian County Council took over the park.

The opening of the park took place in the middle of the big strike of 1926. In other parts of the country, Fife in particular, there were violent

General view taken at the opening of the Welfare Park in 1926.

Lord Chelmsford, chairman of the Welfare Commission, speaking at the park opening. Mungo Mackay is seated directly behind him.

Lord Chelmsford posing in the children's playground with three school pupils.

View of the children in the playground with the new primary school behind.

Newbattle Bowling Green, Newtongrange.

Victoria Park, home ground of Newtongrange Star F.C.

Mary Allan being crowned Gala Queen by Mrs. Fowler, wife of the headmaster of Newbattle School, in the Square.

The putting green in the Welfare Park. The embankment at the bottom of the park carried the colliery railway to the White Gates. There were two tunnels under the railway giving access to the park.

scenes during the strike but there was little trouble in Newtongrange. Union leaders were present at the park opening, notably Andrew Clarke, who was later to be President of the Scottish Miners. In his speech he commented that, "If the standard of life throughout the country had been regulated by the standard of the social amenities that had been provided in Newtongrange, they would probably not have had the measure of unhappiness that had been prevailing throughout the country during the last 19 weeks."

John Purves, the Dean manager since 1916, went away to Stirling in 1924, where he had bought a pub. The Committee spoke to Tom Hackett, who was then manager at the Bottom Shop, and engaged him as manager of the Dean. Big Bob McKinlay was the second man. Jim Barton recollects, "When Hackett went in he sent for me, for spare time after that. So ah went wi Hackett an a wis there for eleeven year.

They didnae bottle much beer up at the Dean. It was mair boucht in there. But we bottled some beer. Ye hid Barclay Perkins. We washed oor ain bottles and then they got 1d. when they broucht them back. There wis nae heavy beer or lager. There were nane o' that - a' draught light and draught stout. There were nae taps like the present day. The pumps worked by pressure, a water engine.

Ye had different brands o' whisky in the Dean -Crawford's three star and Crawford's five star. They had their own whisky tae, the Dean Special. They had it in jars, twae gallon jars on the bar - ye got a nip oot the jar. It wis in bottles tae. During the Second War ye were only allowed two nips on Saturday nicht.

Ladies wid come intae the joog bar and sit. Then they wid come in tae get a pint o' beer for their man wi' a tin pitcher or a cheeny jug. Ye put it in an' just geen them an extra pu' - 6d. a pint, same as through the bar.

If ye wis teetotal ye could hae a gless o' port. Sherry wis never much asked for. In later years when the weemin was allowed in then it was gin an' vodka an' a' this.

When Baillieston bate Nitten 3-0 in the Scottish Cup, that's the day we sellt eleven hoggets o' beer.* We opened in the mornin', it wis a Saturday mornin' an' ah wis workin'.

Hackett went an' tellt MacKay that ah wis needed so ah came up the

* 4,750 pints

pit at 12 o' clock an' ah wis hame an' washed an' had ma denner an' a wis in the bar when the train cam' in at the back o' yin o' clock. We had a special licence a' day. Ah've never seen anythin' like it. If ye hidnae a tumbler ye couldnae get a drink. Ye couldnae get in an' ye couldnae get oot. Oh, heavens! Yer apron wis wet, yer breaks wis wet, yer drawers wis wet. We hid tae gaun hame and chinge oorselves and come back and get the work din. There wernae even a drink for the waiters.

The Dean wis wild at times. We yist tae hae fights regular. Ah got the seck for fightin' three or fower times." Once Jim Barton spilled beer on a man, Sammy Hay. Sammy hit him so Jim hit him back. "He went strecht ower the table. He wis unconscious. Ah hid tae take him hame on the barry. So MacKay go tae ken aboot that an' ah got the seck. Well, the brewery yist tae supply us wi' bits wi' string soles on them – canvas. Ah wis stannin' ootside. Hackett comes up tae me. 'Ye'd better bring thae bits back tae the shop'. Ah said, 'If ye want thae bits back came up tae the hoose and get them.' So he says, 'Ye's better come back.' The man admitted he wis wrong an' we wis great pals efter that."

Mr. Barton remembers a break-in at the Dean and the culprit tried to frame him by leaving a trail of Woodbines all the way to his house. They got the man coming off the Glasgow train with a bag of coppers in his pocket. He dropped some of his loot by the side of the road and Chipper Young found it – three pints of whisky in a parcel.

Jim Barton is proud of his knack of carrying fourteen pint mugs of beer by the handles without spilling any. It has won him quite a few bets in his time.

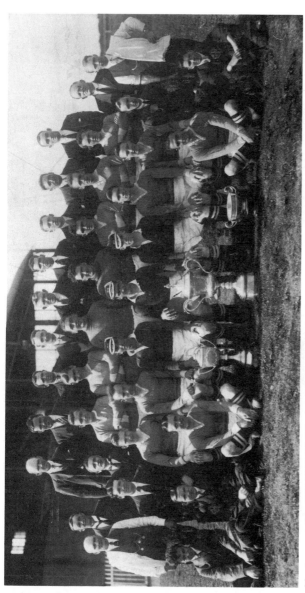

Newtongrange Star F.C. 1929-30. Winners of the Scottish Junior Cup. Back row: (L to R) Wm. Cornwall, Thos. Moffat, Sam McCord, Thos. Naysmith, Robt. Henderson. Alex. Spence. David Jack, Wm. Marshall. 2nd. back row: Walter Greenhill, George Richardson, John Walker, Adam B. Allan, Wm. Petrie. James G. Currie, Geo. Letham. Andrew Wright, Geo. McIntosh, Wm. A. Smith (trainer). Front row: John Kerr, Wm. Torrance, Wm. Walker, Albert Marman, Arthur Todd, Peter S. Henderson (captain), John McPherson, Thos. Young, James D. Barclay, Alex Crichton (secy.), Alex. Reid.Seated ground: J. Kirkwood, S. Moffat, John Thomson, James L. McAulay, W. Cornwall.

Newtongrange Silver Band, 1939. John Rutherford, president, centre front.

Pre-war office workers at the Lothian Coal Company. Back row: (L to R) Jas. Taylor, M. Smith, R. Murray, R. Burnett, A. Crichton, W. Purves, Jim Reid. Middle row: R. Smith, W. Gardner, A. Gardiner, M. Webster, J. Knight, S. Scott, A. McIntosh, J. Burns. Front row: J. Liddle, J. Gilmour, D. Erskine, J. C. Murray, A. Naysmith, P. Bourhill, J. Davis, J. Young.

A dramatic moment in the play, 'Hewers of Coal' (1936). L to R: Alex Convery, Jimmy McPherson (behind), John Reid.

Members of the cast outside the picture house just before they left for London for the British Finals of the One-Act Play Festival (1937).

Top of the village, 1930's, with picture house and Jenny Scott's shop on the left.

Burgari Quinto organised the sale of Sunday newspapers in Newtongrange and he is pictured here with his paper laddies. :

Chapter 12

The Village In The Thirties

The miners in Newtongrange were given a choice in 1932 - bathrooms and back kitchens or pithead baths. They voted for bathrooms and pithead baths were not build until the 1950s. Midlothian County Council began building houses in the village in 1933 and the first street completed was called Gardiner's Crescent after Sandy Gardiner, the popular chairman of Newbattle District Council. Old Abbeyland, dating from the 1840s, contained the oldest miner's houses in the village and these were demolished about 1933. The Lothian Coal Co. was clearing the ground for what was to be their final housebuilding scheme in Newtongrange, Galadean. Newtongrange House was by this time a derelict shell, having lain empty since 1924, when the last surviving daughter of John Romans had died. The Coal Co. had bought the house and its few acres from the Trustees and it was demolished. Some of the stone from Newtongrange House was used in the building of shops at the top of the village in the early 1930s.

Burgari Quinto had a chip shop and a cafe, the Midlothian Soda Parlour, at the top of the village and another chip shop and an icecream shop at the other end. Mr. Quinto was the one man in the village who ignored the summons to appear in front of Mungo MacKay's "green table." "Tell MacKay to come and see me," he is reported to have said and there was nothing Mr. MacKay could do. Mr. Quinto owned his own shops and indeed owned most of the other shops at the top of the village. He was beholden to no one in Newtongrange.

There was no Roman Catholic Church in Newtongrange, although there were a considerable number of Catholics in the village. Dalkeith was their nearest church. Newtongrange United Free Church became Church of Scotland in 1929 at the union of the two churches. The Salvation Army had a hall and so did the Ebeneezer Church ('the Tin Kirk'). The other church in the village was the Church of Christ, which was called 'Allan's Church', after Willie Allan, the mining contractor.

There were two paper shops in the village, Syme's and Samuel's. Samuel's was near the Dean and the paper laddies vied with each other to be first in the shop at night to collect the evening papers. The first one

105

out always made for the Dean where he could easily sell seven or eight dozen on a Saturday night. The *Evening News* was by far the more popular. The *Dispatch* came a very poor second. The *Daily Herald* was the daily paper most in demand in the '30s with the *Daily Express* not far behind.

The first person in Samuel's shop every morning was Johnnie Gilmour, the chief wages clerk at the pit. He cycled up on his way to his work from Lothian Bridge and came in for the Colliery Office papers at 5 a.m. every morning.

Mr. Syme and Mr. Samuel got the Institute newspaper order six months each at a time. It was a good order - the Institute got a lot of papers and they were read avidly by the older men, particularly. There had to be total silence in the Reading Room, and in the Billiards Room, too. Jack Davies, the caretaker, was very strict. Billiards was one of the main things then apart from football.

Jim Reid recalls, "They had dominoes up in the Institute, there. They had a huge dominoes room. Ye see, they started tae gamble an' the authorities wisnae too pleased about it. At the holidays the men had maybe a pound or twa in their pocket an' there was one or two went down the Institute and by the time they came out there was maybe nae pound at a'. Well, a pound or a couple o' pound was really something. So the authorities really frowned on the gambling. They did stop it to a certain extent.

There wis pitch an' toss. Oh, ah went doon the wids as a laddie because ye could hear them talkin' an they would be jist be in a clearin', a wee clearin' below a tree. They just stood roond aboot. The mair there was, the bigger the kitty. Somebody would say, 'Ah've got the toss.' They put two pennies on their finger and tossed them up and if ye got two heads you've cleaned the rink and if ye got one head and one tail ye got another throw and if ye got two tails ye wis out, ye wis beaten. They wid say,

'Ah'll hae 2/-.'

'Ah'll hae 10/-.'

'Ah'll cover that an' ah'll cover that. Well look ah'm cleaned oot ah, canny cover any mair.' If ye couldnae get yer bet on that wis too bad. ye had a winnin' steak ye could jist say, 'Well look, ah'll hiv' another birl. If yer wantin' yer money back ye'd better get it in now.' Ye jist threw yer pennies tae somebody else. It wisnae big money, of course. They wisnae paid big money then. But it's died out. Ah never see anybody playin' that now.

In the auld days the bookies had a man standin' at the Institute. Now, whenever he saw the police he scuttered intae the Institute. They knew, the police knew, that he was collectin' bets so it was maybe yince in six months they lifted him. The bookie was Johnnie Banks o' Bonnyrigg an' there wis a chap frae Loanhead. It was a local miner here, that stood. He was on the night shift. Of course, the bookies would bring across the lines that had won an' he stood there till maybe the racin' finished. Tucker Bennett they called him. He was on it for years and years.

Thomas Strang had the first football pools. He was just a wee bookie - he started somewhere in Rosewell or Bonnyrigg but he gradually grew an' grew. No' the money that they get now, of course, maybe £500 or £1,000. It was a' fixed odds. Ah remember one he had. It was 12 results an' ye had tae mark 1, 2, X. It wisnae 8 draws, as it is now, tae win a million pounds. If ye had the 12 results up, well ye wis on a good thing but if ye had 11 that was nae good. An' then gradually in comes Littlewoods and Zetters an' then they made the gamblin' legal. They got a shop here an' a shop there, ye see."

Football was the biggest interest for most of the miners. Jim Reid says, "They were a' fitba daft. Anywhere ye could get eleven men together ye had a team an' ye entered intae a juvenile league. The main thing that every miner wanted was tae draw on the blue jersey of Nitten Star. Ah've seen in the opening league match they always drew Arniston at home or Arniston away an' ah remember walkin' up the braes frae here tae auld Newbyres Park. If there was one person there, there would be two thousand five hundred of a gate - 3d. in tae see the match. Ye never referred tae them, that ye wis playin' Arniston Rangers football club. Ye wis playin' 'the Germans'. Ah think it was a relic o' the First World War. Sometimes they ca'd us 'the Chinks' or the Nitten Bills [Bulls]. Auld Arniston folk yist tae say, 'How are ye daein', Bill?'"

Arniston folk were also called 'the Square Heids' but there was never any real animosity.

The Burns Club had a good drama club in the 1930s. George Humphrey was the producer and he got Joe Corrie, a Fife miner and playwright, to write a one-act play for the club. 'Hewers of Coal' was entered into the Scottish Community Drama Association One-Act Play Festival in 1936 and won the Scottish Final at Inverness. This got them through to the British Finals at the Old Vic Theatre in London in May 1937. This is an extract from the programme:

NEWBATTLE BURNS CLUB DRAMATIC SOCIETY
"HEWERS OF COAL"
By JOE CORRIE

Sandy (a miner)	ADAM HALDANE
Willie (a pony driver)	JAMES T BAIN
Peter (a pit handyman)	ALEX CONVERY
Bob (the Gaffer)	JOHN MCPHERSON
Ned (a miner)	JOHN REID
Wireless Announcer	GEORGE MCPHERSON
Chorus and Noises off	JAMES MILLER,
	TOM HUMPHREY,
	ANDREW BLACK

Scene 1: Underground
Scene 2: An old "Heading"
Time: The Present
Produced by GEORGE HUMPHREY
Assisted by ROBERT FINLAY
Stage Manager: DAVID JONES

Adam Haldane remembers, "In the actual play we wore oor pit claes. Oor make-up was coal stoor, except for a wee bit lipstick and a bit o' red in the corner o' the eyes. In the final oo was criticised for talkin' in Scots. The adjudicators said it would have been better in an English dialect so the folk could have understood it! Well, it was aye oor contention, we might have been wrong, that the cup went tae the North of England as it had never been there before. It was no' long efter the War that the club broke up. The TV kinna put a stop tae it. The young yins wasnae interested."

The other drama club in the village was started up by Sandy Noble. One time they did a production of 'Brandy Andy' and they had a realistic looking bar made up at the pit for the set. The club borrowed all the props from the Dean including half a dozen big bottles of 'Dalkeith'. Only the till was not real.

In 1935 there were three thousand men employed at the three New-battle pits, Lady Victoria, Lingerwood and Easthouses. Most of the men worked at the Lady Vic. Anderson Duncan says, "It wis a guid pit tae work in, the Lady. We hid oor bad times, tae, but ye got through. We hid some laughs - no mony - mair sweerin' than anythin'! Ye got yer fun on a Friday night. A couple o' pints and 20 Capstan for a couple o' bob. Takin' it all in all, it wis a pretty good village."

Although the miners lived in Lothian Coal Co. houses most of them were not employed directly by the Coal Co. but by individual contractors. George Armstrong recalls, "Ye worked tae a contractor. The contractors paid ee. They were paid well, right enough, but the men were only gettin' pandrops. Ah worked tae him that has the garage up at the Toll, there, Willie Allan. He wis a hard taskmaster, tae."

Some of the men worked a pool system called 'penny a boot'. Anderson Duncan remembers, "Ye appointed a man from yer ain crowd tae look efter things. He collected the pays at one o' clock on a Friday and made them up. Ye had ten men - maybe one or two o' them old men. If somebody wis in a bad bit and you were in a good bit an' if ye were loused early, ye went in tae help. There wis mair comradeship then. Ye had tae work harder. The union had nae say at a'. If ye got the seck ye had tae flit."

Mungo MacKay could sack anyone over the head of the contractors and they had to be out of their house within 24 hours. The Lothian Mine Owners kept a blacklist and if you were on it you might not get a job in another Lothian pit. No other coal company in the Lothians had such tight control over their work force as the Lothian Coal Co. had. Some men found it oppressive. Hector McNeil worked there for a time but he hated it. He used to say, "The dugs in New York are barkin' the name o' the Lothian Coal Company!"

The Lothian Coal Co, however, never had any difficulty in getting men to work at Newbattle. Ever since the company had been formed in 1890, it had been their intention to build good houses to attract steady workmen. There were huge coal reserves at Newbattle and the Lothian Coal Co. was prepared to invest very large sums of money on developing the Lady Victoria Pit to ensure future company profits. Building good houses was part of this plan, although the cost of the housing was minimised by cheap Government loans and clever accounting.

The Lothian Coal Co. was far ahead of other coal owners in this matter. Housing for miners was generally so bad in Britain that a Housing Commission had been set up in 1912 to investigate conditions. Miner's leader, Robert Brown, called the Newtongrange houses, "probably the best houses built for miners in Scotland."

The establishment of the Dean Tavern in 1899 was intended to regulate drinking in the village and to create profits to provide amenities in Newtongrange and Easthouses. To some extent these aims conflicted and the management were well aware of it. Company chairman, Mr. Hood, had stated at the opening of the bowling green in 1902 that, "The company felt that by establishing this public house it would be the means of repressing drinking – drunkenness certainly – because they offered no encouragement to drink." And further, "... I have heard it suggested that it would be an inducement for people to spend money in consideration that they would derive some benefit from it. Personally, I would be very glad if the profits from the public-house were to diminish rather than increase, provided the reason was a diminution of drunkenness."

The Dean Tavern made large profits which provided Newtongrange with a wide range of amenities at no cost to the Lothian Coal Co. Indeed, some of the directors benefited handsomely by lending large sums of money to the Dean Committee at 5% interest (a good rate then).

The Lothian Coal Co, represented by the notorious figure of general manager, Mungo MacKay, was able to exert control to a unique degree over the lives of its employees. Historian, Ian MacDougall, writes "Authoritarian colliery managers were commonplace in the days of the coalmasters, but none of Mungo MacKay's contemporaries appears to have earned quite so much notoriety among Scots miners as he did. His autocratic methods, ruthlessly applied, gave him control not only over the pits around Newtongrange but the pubs, the churches, the people and whole villages." (Odyssey, 1982)

Midlothian miners had never been conspicuously militant at any time and the Marquis of Lothian was able to control his work force closely before the days of the Lothian Coal Co. By providing good housing, steady work and a well-regulated village the Lothian Coal Co. was able to be very fussy about whom they would employ. Naturally, they took on men they thought would fit in with the system that Mungo MacKay had so successfully established.

Two of the Dean waiters, Andrew Aikman (left) and Bob McKinlay (right) with three customers.

Barclay Perkins label for stout bottled at the Dean. Jim Barton has kept this label for forty years.

A set of very interesting photographs from an early Gala Day.

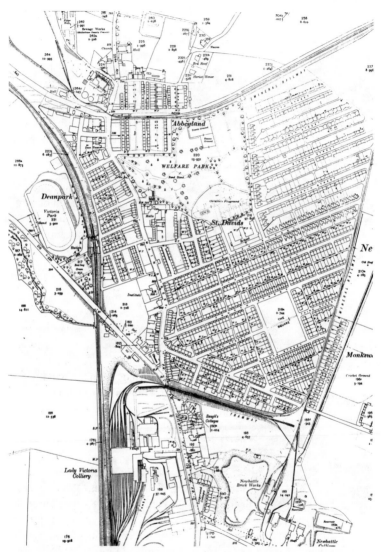

Newtongrange, 1934. The Lothian Coal Company's house-building schemes were now completed. Midlothian County Council began building council houses in 1933 to the north-east of the village.

Chapter 13

The Dean in the Thirties

Tom Hackett was the manager of the Dean Tavern until 1934 when got the sack as the Committee had heard he was applying for a licence elsewhere. At the same time Bob McKinlay was sacked as he had been seen under the influence of drink in the Dean. Mr. Hackett took the Argyle Bar in Leith Street and later had the Central Bar at the bottom of Leith Walk.

The Dean Committee sent for Andrew Aikman to see if he would be manager. He had begun at the Dean as a boy in 1925 and left in 1932 when he was second man, to take over as manager at Hamilton Lodge in Portobello. He was still only 24 when he came back to the Dean. He was to get £3 a week and Tony Docherty, who was engaged as second man, got £2 a week.

Willie Yuill, the present manager of the Dean, recalls, "22 years ah worked for him and Andrew Aikman was really a publican among publicans. He was a man of foresight. When he came here as manager, he saw that the Dean had to move and he changed the Dean. He told me there was big wooden tables and forms. There were no curtains in the windows - nothing. 'Why should the miner be different from anyone else?' It was a stone floor - a terrazzo floor. He went on to lay a floor of lino. He brought in tables and chairs. He put blinds up in the windows. I learned a lot from him. He taught me a lot. He was near teetotal. Ah've seen the man take a sherry on occasion but he never drank in the pub. He never drank locally. Andrew Aikman was a family man. He was popular with the authorities. He ran a good place. He was a very benevolent man. He was good to the old people - very popular among old people. To me Andrew Aikman was a perfect publican."

Anderson Duncan remembers, "Ye came in the Dean, 'Wha's beer is it?' It didnae mak' much difference. We drank it just the same. Three or four pints and we were happy." Jim Reid says, "Ah remember my father tellin' me. He could tell whenever Deuchar's beer was in. He said it was great and then the second best was McLennan and Urquart of Dalkeith. Well they're both gone now. Beer was a tanner a pint. Three pints and ye knew you'd had a drink. Ah don't think the beer is now what it was. If ye wanted a drink on a Sunday ye had tae gaun up tae Lauder or that - bona fide traveller, passing through."

John and Tom Lockhart recall, "It wis a' pints they bought. There wernae much whisky then. It wis a' pints. They yist tae say the miners washed the stoor away. There wis nae heavy beer in the Dean or the Bottom Shop. It wis a' light beer. Ye jist asked fir a pint. The Abbey Inn was aye Youngers, Robert Youngers o' Abbeyhill. The Dean had different beers. If they tain the coal that's hoo they tain the beer. They jist geen ye onythin'."Jim Reid: "John Gilmour was the chief wages clerk up there but he was also secretary of the Dean Committee an' he yist tae crack tae me aboot the Dean, ye know, and what they did - it was barter in a way. All right, you buy two waggons (20 ton) of our coal tae keep ee goin' and we'll take x number of hogsheads of your beer. They were always good quality beers.

In those days it was barrels - a hogshead or a barrel, or a half barrel. Now it's a' these tin things. Well, they can bump them off, put them up and serve in practically an hour after, but ye couldnae do that wi' a barrel o' beer. Ye had tae tae knock the wee thing tae let it seep, you know, an' if ye did it at the wrong time, or the barrel had been badly shaken up, ye didnae get a good pint o' beer."

Anderson Duncan remembers, "The Bottom Shop had a better cellar than the Dean. The Dean wisnae a whisky shop, it wis a beer shop. It wis jist the auld men that drunk whisky then."

John and Tom Lockhart: "Ah think when ah startit drinkin' it wis 6d. a pint and 7d. a nip. If ye wantit Special it wis 8d. When a' went an' asked for the Dean whisky - an' it's the end bottle this side, it's aye the end bottle. It's a different brand - every wee while it's a different brand o' whisky. It's cheaper. It's no their ain brand. They yist tae buy that whisky in bulk an' bottle it thersel' and the same wi' the sherry. They cried it Dean Cream. Till they got fed up an' got it bottled fir them."

Jim Reid recalls, "Originally the miner liked to stand with his feet in the sawdust. Maist o' the miners smoked a pipe and it just ** intae the sawdust - and it caught spilled beer too."

George Armstrong: "It's changed. An awfu' lot o' the auld yins went tae the Dean. It's the younger element now." John and Tom Lockhart: "There's hardly ony miners in the Dean now - a' miners then."

116

Jim Reid: "200 men ye got intae the Dean - a' in wee groups and thir only conversation, strangely enough, was their work. There's more faces been worked and roads back brushed in the Dean Tavern than anywhere else."

There was an alcove in the public bar called 'the manhole'. Jim Reid: "The manhole was where the local worthies congregated." Alec Trench: "Oo cried them the manholes because the miners a' sat in there an' howked coal and brushed roads an' that. Ye ken, every night when they were havin' a crack."

Katherine McKerrow writes, "The Dean played a big part in the lives of the "Nitten" folk as we were called. It was our meeting place over the years but with one difference. We were on the outside, not inside. What I want to tell you about is my grandpa. He started work in the Lady Victoria, at the age of 13 and retired at 65. His life being when he was finished work and washed in front of the fire. After his dinner - down to the Dean where he had one seat, he never sat on any other. We knew where to get him. Every night Granny and I had to go down to the jug bar at the side with the wee pitcher and get it filled - one pint every night. When Gran took ill I got the job, every night, which I carried out for many years. The high spots for me were on a Saturday night, when Grandpa would bring me a comb or hair grips or any small thing, but he never forgot me on the Saturday. A gentleman with a case used to come into the Dean selling small items. My mother also met my dad coming from a dance. He was outside of the Dean and chatted Mother up."

Masterton House, Newtongrange, a 17th. century fortified laird's house. Demolished 1942.

Peter Watson seated on the Dean van in 1958.

Spectators at a Newtongrange Star v. Arniston Rangers match in the 1940s.

Sandy Gardiner, Chairman of Newbattle District Council laying the foundation stone of the council offices, 28th. July 1937. The man in plus fours is Archie Dougall, the registrar.

The juvenile pipe band at a contest.

Some Newtongrange men on a Dean drive having reached their destination. Frank Taylor, the Company policeman is second right at the back.

Refreshment stop on a Dean Drive.

Customers at the jug bar, 1949. L to R: Jimmy Tosh, Willie Landels, Tootie Bain, Charlie Smith, Alex. Pow.

Free beer at the Dean on the night of 29th. October 1949, provided by Murrays the brewers to celebrate 50 years of the Dean.

Chapter 14

The Last Forty Years.

The Dean Committee had bought an empty church in the village in 1939. The congregation of Newtongrange Parish Church had completed their new hall and were using it for worship until the church was built. The Dean intended to let the drams club use the old church and the boy scouts to use the former church hall but the outbreak of war prevented this. The old church was used as a British Restaurant during the War and in 1946 it was sold to the Masons, who had shared the Band Hall with the silver band until then.

Andrew Aikman was called up in 1940 and his wife managed the Dean in his absence. Alex Menzies was put in charge of the cellar. Of the two barmen, Tom Reid joined the Guards and John Lockhart was called up. For the first time a barmaid, Jessie Robson served at the Dean.

The profits for the first three years of the war were between £1,200 and £1,500 but in 1943 they fell to £550 in what was "the worst statement for over 40 years." 1945 was another very bad year but in the first full financial year after the war (1945-1946) profits reached the record level of £4,800.

The most significant event of 1947 was the transfer of the coal mines in Britain from private ownership to public ownership. This took place on 'Vesting Day', January 1st. Anderson Duncan: "Everythin' was tae be a bed o' roses but it was still the same team in different jerseys. There was nae difference until they brought in mechanisation. Nationalisation was a good thing right enough, when ye got guaranteed wages. A lot o' them could of worked harder, though."

The Lothian Coal Co. continued for a further five years to wind up its affairs. Their lawyers asked to see the books of the Dean Tavern in 1948 to find out if the Dean owed the Coal Co. any money. Details of the final payment were found and the lawyers were satisfied that the Coal Co. had no legal claim on the Dean.

The Dean celebrated its 50th anniversary in 1949 and, on the 29th of October, there was free beer to celebrate the occasion for the customers supplied by Murray's Brewery. Remarkably, John Gilmour had been clerk to the Dean Committee all those years.

The Committee Members at this time were George MacKay, who had been appointed on the death of his father, Mungo, in 1939, David Haldane, William Darge, John Ross and Andrew Aikman. Mr. Aikman, as manager, had a full-time bar staff of six in 1949. There was Tom Reid, head barman, Gerry Daly, Ben Daly, Tom Haylott, Willie Mitchell, who stoked the boilers, and an eighteen year old called William Yuill, who had just come from the Hunterfield Goth.

There had always been bad feeling between the Dean and the Welfare Committees. The Dean felt that the Welfare was asking them for too much money and the Welfare thought the Dean was refusing to pay money that was due to them. In 1948, after a dispute over payments, the Welfare secretary wrote to the Dean Committee alleging that the Dean owed them £4,000. The Committee consulted their solicitor who said they had no case to answer. Accounts were produced to show that the Welfare had received almost £20,000 over the previous 24 years, an average of £830 a year. The Welfare also received a levy on every ton of coal produced at Newbattle and 3d. a week for each miner. Out of this they had to maintain the park, pay the district nurse, maintain the two Institutes and the two bands.

In 1950, the Welfare Park was taken over by the County Council and this saved the Dean hundreds of pounds a year. The Welfare people frequently asked to see the Dean's accounts, their constitution and for representation of the Dean Committee. All these requests were turned down. In 1954, John Rutherford, a life-long trade union official and a man who had been involved with the Newbattle Welfare since its beginning, was asked to be a member of the Dean Commmittee. He was not, however, officially representing the Welfare

Mr. Rutherford certainly livened up the Dean Committee meetings. He asked for more meetings, for more details about the accounts and he persistently pressed for a formal constitution for the Committee. Talks about a constitution had begun in 1952, when a Q.C. had been consulted, but the issue took many years to resolve.

The Welfare was getting further into debt after the war and, in 1949, asked for help from the Dean to pay off a loss of £1,000, run up by the pit canteen during the war. The Dean turned down this request and sent a lawyer's letter to say so.

The Dean had owned the Institutes at Newtongrange at Easthouses until 1943 when it was arranged to sell them to the Welfare. Extensive repairs were needed and Central Welfare funds were only available for buildings belonging to them. The two Institutes were valued at £8,250, altogether, and the Dean planned to spend the money on houses for retired miners. However, no money was ever paid to the Dean although the Welfare became the owners.

In 1952 the Miner's Welfare organisation was re-organised under the title of the Coal Industry Social Welfare Organisation (C.I.S.W.O.). The central body was funded by a grant from the National Coal Board. Miners pay a voluntary levy for the upkeep of local Welfare schemes, including institutes and clubs.

In the mid 1950s, Newbattle District Council, C.I.S.W.O. and the Education Committee of Midlothian County Council gave a joint grant to build a large hall at the Institute. At the same time, Newtongrange Community Association was formed to manage the former Institute and the new hall, which together were called Newtongrange Community Centre. Membership of the Community Centre was 6d. a week for miners and non-miners, alike. The only difference being, the miners had 6d. deducted from their wages every week (although they could opt out) and this gave them access to billiards, dominoes and the reading room. The public library was also in the building and was run by the Education Committee.

It transpired that the membership fees were insufficient to cover the running costs and the District Council had to bail them out two or three times. Finally, it was agreed that Newbattle District Council should take over the building and it was sold to them for 1/-. John Jenks, one of the councillors, recalls, "The miners felt the District took the Institute from them but, in actual fact, we saved it for them. The District Council spent quite a lot of money on the building."

Financial troubles continued to plague the Community Association and a meeting was arranged with the Dean Committee to seek support from them.

A special Meeting was convened for 15th July 1967 at 3 p.m. to receive a deputation from the Trustees of the Newtongrange Welfare Institute.

Composition of the Meeting:

For the Institute	For the Dean Tavern Committee
Mr Steel	Mr MacKay, Chairman
Mr Bannerman	Mr Ross
Mr Arthur	Mr Aikman
Mr Coyle	Mr Currie,
Secretary Mr Cowan	Mr Morgan

Mr Cowan spoke for the Institute on its financial position, pointing out that unless it received immediate financial aid it would in the meantime have to close down. They, in order to keep going, required an immediate sum of £600 to pay off their outstanding debt and promise of continuing financial aid. They had decided that if this was not forthcoming from the Dean, they had no alternative but to carry on with a proposal to go forward with a scheme of using a part of their premises for the purposes of a Licensed Club. The discussion then became general, during which the Dean Secretary pointed out that the Dean was not at present in a position to grant this aid, in view of large sums which, in recent years, had been spent on making the Dean more modern in the Bars and adding a Function Hall to the already large premises. Mr Cowan conceded that it was very obvious that the affairs of the Dean had been well managed, a remark to which there was no disagreement. Mr Steel, who represented the District Council, indicated that so far as he knew that body would not assist financially in the meantime. The Dean Committee regretted their inability to assist them in the meantime." (Dean Committee Minute Book)

The Community Association got a club licence in 1967 and re-named the premises Newtongrange Community Association Social Club (generally known as the 'Top Club', as they are at the top end of the village). The Community Association is now more or less defunct and the club is run by a committee.

The Dean had had a virtual monopoly in Newtongrange since 1899 but after World War Two competition developed from licensed clubs. Jim Reid says, "Mind you the Dean wasnae pleased when a' these licences got up, ye know. Ye see, it was takin' custom - and the worst blow was the Morris Club. John Morris was a rabid Labour councillor, despite the fact he had a shop. Some o' the men went tae him, 'We'll have tae get some place else tae drink. We'll have tae break away frae the Dean.' It was that crowded on a Saturday night." The Morris Club took

Bernard's beer and in retaliation the Dean stopped buying Bernard's beer, even though it was a good seller.

The Bowling Club wanted a club licence in 1947 and they needed the agreement of the Dean, which still owned the green and pavilion. George MacKay supported their application and he convinced the other Committee members that it was a good idea. The Bowling Club got its licence. In 1979, the Bowling Club negotiated a 40 year lease with the Dean Tavern and the club now manage their own affairs entirely.

The British Legion also got a club licence and, in 1958, the Star got a licence - without the blessing of the Dean. The Star park and pavilion had been handed over to the football club in 1948, as the Dean were anxious to get rid of a property, which had cost them thousands since it was built in 1924. There were three conditions: (1) There was to be no dog racing (2) The Club was to use the Dean for refreshment sales and (3) The Park and pavilion were to be returned to the Dean if the Star failed. At the same time the Dean Committee gave the Star a loan of £200 for ground repairs. When the star got their licence the Dean asked for the loan to be repaid. A rumour current at the time had it that the Dean had 'fined' the Star £200 for opening a club.

Three public houses had opened in the neighbourhood in the 1940s. John Black got a licence at Newtonloan Toll in 1946; Peter Robertson opened the Sun Hotel in 1948 and Andrew Aikman became licencee of the Barley Bree at Easthouses in 1949. Mr Aikman brought Bernard Daly from the Dean to be his manager and remained as Dean manager himself.

The Dean, for the first time in its history had to attract customers and a modern lounge bar was created in the upstairs room. When a TV was installed there in 1951 the takings increased by £30 a week.

A vast new council housing scheme was being built on the side of the hill above Newtongrange at this time. The National Coal Board were building modern pits at Bilston Glen and Monktonhall and Midlothian County Council were constructing over 1,000 houses at Mayfield to house the incoming miners. They came mainly from the West of Scotland, where old mines were being closed down.

Usher's brewery built a pub in Mayfield (the Country Girl) and the Dean applied for the licence but the licence was granted to David Cochrane instead. The Dean never took Usher's beer after that.

The Dean Committee had plans for a pub at the West end of the village in the 1950s to combat competition from the clubs. It was intended to build above the corner shop ('Jenny Scotts') next to the picture house and the proposed premises were to be called the 'Club Bar'. The idea was to catch the men coming down from the pit. Mr. Twatt who owned the shop objected bitterly, but the Committee had reserved the right to build above the shop when they had sold it. The committee applied for a licence first in 1956, in the name of committee member, David Haldane, and were turned down. A second application in the name of Willie Yuill, barman, was refused in 1957 and a third application in manager, Andrew Aikman's name was also refused in 1959.

The court had no obligation to give reasons for their refusal but privately it was said that there were sufficient licences in the village and that the proposed premises were on the corner of two busy, converging roads. Willie Yuill thinks the Council were against the Dean and says, "The council thought the Dean weren't doing sufficient to let the people know what they were doing."

With the failure of their attempt to build a second pub at the top of the village, the Dean Committee turned their attention to their own premises and a large extension was built in 1962. The *Evening Dispatch* reported,"TAVERN HAS BROUGHT CHANGES IN DRINKING HABITS Great changes in drinking habits have been witnessed by the chairman of the Dean Tavern Trust, Councillor Andrew Aikman. Councillor Aikman started serving in the pub as a boy of 14. He has now 39 years service with it, including 12 as the licensee. Some indication of the respect in which the trustees are held in the village may be gathered from the fact that Mr Aikman was returned as the only independent councillor in a village which is overwhelmingly a Labour stronghold.

Mr Aikman recalls the day when women used to creep into the old jug bar, push a jug across the counter to be filled with beer, and whisper "A nip and a half-pint". Today the womenfolk join their husbands for a quiet drink in the attractively furnished cocktail bar - as swish as anything Edinburgh has to offer-or for a dance in the functions hall on a Saturday night.

"We very, very seldom have any drunks here", Councillor Aikman told me, "but when we do see that they are taken home."

The first day of the new upstairs lounge in the Dean (1951).

New Year's Day in the Dean, early 1970s. Bar staff (L to R): Andrew McIntosh, John Steel, Willie Yuill and Dave Ferguson.

In 1952 a lot of trophies were won by Newtongrange individuals and organisations. They were assembled in the Dean (along with some from previous years) for this picture, flanked by Tom Reid (left) and Andrew Aikman.

A Dean function, early 1950s.

Enjoying a pint in a 'manhole'. L to R: Bob Herriot, Peter Beveridge, Paddy Manley, Bob Black, Tiger Conlan, Dobie Moffat, Tom Young.

L to R: ?, Sandy Miller, Will Lockhart, Tom Lockhart, John Lockhart, Joe Neilson. This part of the Dean is sometimes called 'the Mason's side'.

Inside the Dean after the alterations in 1962.

Draught beer still maintains its place as the most popular drink. It is sold at 1s 1d a pint compared with the usual 1s 3d. The price to old age pensioners is even cheaper 11d.

Bottle beer is also cheaper, and an export is sold to old age pensioners for 1s.

"The reason we are doing this," said Councillor Aikman is because the customers have after all made possible all the various schemes which we have helped to finance. We felt they themselves should have some concession.

Newtongrange has two public-houses including the Dean and seven clubs. It seems rather odd that the seven clubs are open on a Sunday while the Dean, which has done so much to help the welfare of the people of the village remains closed. "If it was left to the customers we'd certainly be open on Sundays," commented Councillor Aikman.

The people of Newtongrange are very proud of the place said Mr W. Yuill charge hand. "The public bar is a real man's bar."

It certainly must be one of the largest and best-stocked in the Edinburgh area. The four trustees of the Dean are Councillor Aikman, Mr George MacKay, son of an original trustee; Mr David Haldane, a retired mining engineer; and Mr John Rutherford a retired trade union official. The secretary is Mr Norman Currie, of Caledonian Breweries.

The £20,000 alterations to the premises have converted them into an attractive, cleverly designed roadhouse with a wineshop (orders are delivered by van to customers), lounge bar, functions hall and dance floor, with bar, games room and public bar."

There was a big controversy before the extension was opened. Willie Yuill: "When they did the alterations they'd no room to store coal or coke so they decided to heat by gas. Well, that caused a furore! From then on the unions came down on us. There were some of them. then, threatened a boycott because we were using gas."

An offer had been made to buy the picture house in 1947 but the Committee turned it down. The picture house was doing very well after the War and the Committee was getting £800 a year in rent from the Burntisland Picture Palace Co. It was decided, however, to sell the shops and flats attached to the picture house and these realised £4,300.

In 1956 the Dean Committee bought, from the Marquis of Lothian, the feu of a piece of ground containing the picture house and all the shops at the top of the village. By an oversight, this did not include the Institute. The Dean was then in a position to prevent any of these premises obtaining a licence in competition to themselves.

Attendances at the picture houses were dwindling and it was closed down in 1962. The County Council bought it with the intention of converting it into a swimming pool but this did not prove feasible. A fine new swimming pool was built in 1969. The picture house is now Jackie Williamson's furniture warehouse.

Members of the Dean Committee had always served for life, with the remaining members choosing a successor on the death of one of them. There had originally been five members but in 1962 there were just four. One member, David Haldane, died in 1965; another Andrew Aikman, resigned in 1965; and a third, John Rutherford, died in 1966. Andrew Ross replaced Mr. Haldane but the other two were not replaced on the advice of Mr. Murray, the lawyer. For the first time, the Dean Tavern was to have a constitution and protracted negotiations were taking place. It was thought that no new Committee members should be appointed until a Trust was formed and Court of Session approval was necessary for this. In 1969, Andrew Ross died leaving George MacKay as the only member of the Committee. For a year and a half Mr. Mac-Kay supervised the running of the Dean himself, visiting the premises every month or two to check the books and sign cheques.

Andrew Aikman, the manager suffered a stroke in August 1970 whilst on holiday and Willie Yuill took over in his absence. Mr Aikman was unable to resume work and resigned on February 5th 1971. He had worked 44 years at the Dean Tavern, 37 of them as manager. He died two months later. Willie Yuill the head barman, who had been running the Dean since the onset of Andrew Aikman's illness, was then appointed manager of the Dean.

A second Committee member, Tom Irvine, was appointed in 1970, as two names were needed on the Court of Session. Finally, in 1971, the constitution was approved and the Dean Tavern Trust was formed. There were to be seven Trustees, as follows:- The chairman and vice - chairman of the South Welfare Sub-Committee of C.I.S.W.O., the chairman of Newtongrange Community Association; the manager of the Bank of Scotland, Dalkeith; a councillor nominated by Newbattle

District Council; and George MacKay and Thomas Irvine who, on their death or resignation, would be replaced by nominees of Newbattle District Council. Meetings must be held at least four times a year and a quorum of five was needed at meetings.

Currently, steps are being taken to alter that part of the Constitution which refers to the appointment of Trustees. It is proposed to have one councillor nominated by Midlothian District Council, one community councillor nominated by Newtongrange Community Council, two people nominated by C.I.S.W.O., the Dalkeith Bank of Scotland manager and two local people nominated by Midlothian District Council. The councillors and the C.I.S.W.O. nominees would serve for three years (as at present) and the two local people for five years and they would all be eligible for re-nomination.

The Dean Tavern Trust is "to apply the whole free profits of the trading carried on, or in connection with, the Dean Tavern for the benefit of the people of Newtongrange and district."

Grants may be given to promote the following objects: "Youth and adult education or training; the study, exposition or practice of the arts; literature, music and drama; sports games and athletics, cultural and recreational activities of all kinds; and the care or recreation of aged, infirm, incapacitated, handicapped or needy persons." Applications for grants are dealt with once a year and have to be made by the end of January. Below is a list of grants awarded in 1986.

Fishing and Flytying Group	£10
Newbattle Community Old Time Dance Section	£10
Newtongrange and Bilston Glen Colliery Pipe Band	£100
Newtongrange Junior Silver Band	£25
Newtongrange Star "A"	£75
Easthouses and Mayfield O.A.P. Association	£100
Newtongrange O.A.P. Association	£100
Darby and Joan Club	£100
Newtongrange Cage Bird Society	£15
Dean Tavern F.C.	£125
Phoenix Youth Club	£275
21st Midlothian Scout Troup	£75
Newtongrange W.R.I.	£15
Gorebridge Police Bowling Section	£10

Debbie Smith	£50
N.C.B.F.C.	£30
Gala Day	£200
Scottish Brewers Silver Band (Newtongrange)	£350
Dean Tavern Darts Club	£25
Newtongrange Accordion and Fiddle Club	£150
Newtongrange Homing Society	£40
Newbattle District Gardening Club	£75
Newtongrange Star Football Club	£100
Newbattle Bowling Club	£100
'The Grange' newsletter	£10
Total	£2165

Mostly, awards are made to groups or societies but occasionally individuals are helped. In 1986 £50 was awarded to Debbie Smith, a talented gymnast, to help with her training expenses.

Alec Trench says, "The Dean's no' changed much since ah started drinkin' there in 1945. It's a lot quieter. Of course it looks quieter but there could be two hunder people in there. Yer lucky if ye see them for there's two lounges and a dance hall and then the big bar. There can be 30 to 40 men sittin' in thon manholes. It's very seldom ye see many men standin' roond the bar nowadays. Ye ken, they get their drink and gaun and sit doon. Before, ye used tae stand at the bar, feet in the sawdust an' that. There's very little o' that anywhere."

Dominoes were first allowed in the Dean in 1934 and the first dartboard was bought in 1941. When the alterations were made in 1962, a large games room was made next to the public bar.

This is an extract from a Committee meeting in December, 1965: "Before the meeting convened the members viewed a new type of Amusement Machine, commonly called a "Fruit Machine" or a One-armed Bandit. Under new regulations it is now quite legal to instal this type of machine in licensed premises. The prizes are strictly limited to one shilling in cash or a disc token valued at 5/- and exchangeable for goods only.

It was finally decided to make formal application to the local Authority for permission to instal this machine on a trial period only."

The darts and dominoes were in the games room and there was also a

135

pinball machine and a football machine but the games room was never very popular. People did not really want to be apart from the rest of the company in the pub and in 1972 the games room was made into a lounge bar.

Alec Trench recalls, "There wis a lot o' cairry oot. There wis the Dean barry jist tae deliver thir orders on a Saturday night. People that wis havin' a cairry oot – maybe a dozen o' them – the Dean barry would take them up tae thir hooses. If ye see somebody half drunk ye'd say, 'Better get the Dean barry!' Ye could borrow it for flittin's."

The Dean barrow was eventually stolen and in 1951 the Dean van made its appearance. It was mainly for carry outs but it was also used to take home drunks.

Gorebridge Store was the only off-licence grocer's shop in the village and the Dean did a great deal of off-sales business, especially at New Year, but the Dean cannot now compete price-wise with supermarkets and cut-price stores.

Willie Yuill recalls that the Dean was mainly a beer shop. "We used to sell 20 barrels of light beer a week, no problem. The breweries all got a turn. Dalkeith might get an order for two hogsheads. McEwans and Murrays might get six hogheads."

The following brewers all supplied the Dean with draught beer:

William Younger	Dalkeith
Aitkens of Falkirk	Bernards
Robert Younger	Ushers
Campbell Hope and King	Tennants
George Younger	McLaughlan
Youngs of Musselburgh	Dryboroughs
Murrays	Fowlers
Lorimer and Clark	Deuchars
McEwans	Aitchisons
Steel, Coulsons	Maclays
Jeffreys	

Beer from two breweries was available at any one time but they were never named. To sell beer from so many breweries was a practice unique to the Dean. Willie Yuill: "The customers wouldn't put up with it nowadays. You were changing a man's palate every week."

Latterly, William Murray and Co. began to get more business than the other breweries, partly because they were the first brewery to deliver locally. Other breweries delivered by train to the nearest station and the order was picked up by a local carrier.

Murray's had guaranteed the bank overdraft at the time of the Dean extension in 1960 and had given the Dean a loan to build the new Bowling Club pavilion in 1962. In return, the Dean made a commitment to take a certain amount of Murray's beer.

In 1962 the Dean Tavern was the first pub in Scotland to have beer delivered in tanks. Willie Yule: "If they could sell it here they could sell it anywhere. This was the test bed." It was at this time that heavy beer became popular and the demand for light beer dropped away.

The large-scale extensions and improvements completed in 1960 had cost £20,000 and this had seriously over stretched the Dean's resources. It took a long time to pay off the overdraft and it was not cleared until the mid 1970s.

Each time a new club had opened in the village the Dean's trade was affected. It largely recovered after a time, but business was not as good as it had been in the past. The biggest blow came when the Top Club opened in 1969 and, for a while, it was very popular, to the detriment of the Dean. At the same time, the Dean had no proper committee, Andrew Aikman took ill and died shortly after and so did the secretary, Norman Currie.

Geoff Craythorne was appointed secretary in 1970 and Willie Yuill took over from Andrew Aikman that year. In 1971, the Dean Trust was formed and from about this time the fortunes of the Dean improved. By 1978, the annual turnover had risen to £125,000 a year, although a lot of that was due to inflation. Since then, trade has been very good and the business is now on a firm footing. For a number of years, some of the profits have been set aside annually to build up a reserve fund. Necessary structural repairs currently taking place to the Dean will cost many thousands of pounds and the whole burden can be met from the reserves. The fabric of the building has deteriorated fairly seriously over the years.

The turnover of the Dean Tavern for the year 1985-86 was £212,000 leaving a net profit of just under £5,000. Of this, just over £2,000 was given out in donations to local organisations and the rest was put into the reserve fund.

The costs of running the Dean are relatively high in comparison to those of other pubs, due to the size of the building. It's a big, rambling place that requires more to heat, light, repair and staff than would a smaller place.

Willie Yuill: "We try to sell drinks as cheap as we possibly can sell them and still keep up the standards. Our drinks prices are the same as the club's - cheaper than other pubs, well below them. My view is the customer should get back a bit more because he's the man who frequents it. The customer should get the benefit. The Christmas gift is a way of thanking the regular customer."

Since 1899 over £1000,000 has been spent by the Dean on village amenities. Most of the profits from the first twenty five years were spent on big projects like the bowling green, the football park, the two Institutes, the picture house and the nurse's cottage, etc. For a few years after that, the Dean's funds were used to maintain the facilities they had provided in the early years. the Welfare Park, the Institutes and the Star Park proved particularly expensive to maintain. Beinning in 1943, the Dean Committee (with hindsight, very wisely) began to divest itself of these properties. Over a number of years, they were able to give away or sell the properties they owned except the Dean itself and the bowling green. The land they were built on, however, still belonged to the Marquis of Lothian and the lease was due to terminate in 1982. One of the first aims of the newly constituted Dean Trust in 1972, therefore, was to secure the lease.

The Lothian Estates asked for £20,000 but eventually the Marquis, on a visit to the Dean, accepted the Trust's offer of £2,000. He said he was happy with the management of the place but wanted a promise that good quality bowling would always continue at the bowling green.

The National Coal Board inherited just over one thousand houses in Newtongrange from the Lothian Coal Co. in 1947. It was the largest coal mining village in Scotland, but the Coal Board never made very great landlords and gradually the houses deteriorated, due to lack of maintenance. There was concern in the village when the Coal Board began moving out tenants in parts of Fourth and Fifth Streets in the early 1970s and demolishing some of the houses. Newtongrange Housing Action Group was formed and representations were made to the N.C.B., the N.U.M., and Midlothian District Council. Newtongrange was then made a Conservation Area and the demolitions stopped. An independent feasability study, commissioned by the Action Group, proved that the houses were structurally sound, though in need of costly **rehabilitation. The N.C.B. had no interest in modernising the houses** as the lease of the land from the Lothian Estates was due to end in 1982. The lease stipulated that the land the houses were built on was to be returned to the Lothian Estates in its original condition and suitable for agricultural use. The District Council were unable to help without Government funding and a general feeling of depression and despair overtook the village. Nevertheless, a survey made by Newtongrange Community Council revealed that the great majority of residents not only wanted to stay in the village but would prefer to have their present houses modified rather than have new houses built.

A significant factor in the campaign was a BBC TV programme about the plight of Newtongrange called 'The Village That Nobody Wants.' This brought home the village's problem to a much wider public.

Eventually the Government intervened and the Housing Corporation compensated Lothian Estates for the land not being returned to agricultural use for an undisclosed sum. The Housing Corporation then bought 116 houses from Lothian Estates for £200,000 and transferred them to Castle Rock Housing Association with a grant for their rehabilitation. A company called Grange Estates is modernising other properties for sale or rent and some houses have been sold privately. A large number of houses have yet to be modernised and more Government money will be needed to complete the work. A private developer is about to begin building a new scheme of up to 100 houses on reclaimed land at Lingerwood Pit.

During the worries over the housing, a major blow to the village had come with the closure of the Lady Vic, the last family pit in Midlothian. Some of the men took redundancy and others transferred to Monkton Hall or Bilston Glen. During its lifetime 39,524,215 tons of coal were wrought from the Lady. It closed on the 27th March 1981, much lamented.

One good thing that has come out of the closure of the Lady is the birth of the Scottish Mining Museum on part of the site. The magnificent steam-operated winding engine has been retained and a display, with re-constructed scenes from village life, has opened in the old Colliery Office. There is a museum shop and a good tea room. The other half of the Mining Museum is at Prestongrange in East Lothian.

The Dean has had some ups and downs over the last thirty years or so. Every time a new club opened (and there are now six) business fell away for a time but usually recovered. The biggest threat, at the time, appeared to be the miner's club (the 'Top Club') when it opened in the old Institute in 1967 but the Dean weathered that storm.

During the 1960s and much of the 1970s, the Dean was saddled with large debts, incurred in the building of the extensions in 1962, but over the past ten years substantial reserves have been built up. Business is good and growing under the ebullient management of Willie Yule. The Trust supports a lot of village societies with annual grants. During the miner's strike of 1984-85, the Dean provided the Women's Support Group with £50 worth of food a week.

The Dean is looking remarkably hale and hearty after its 86th birthday and has a long way to go yet.

Dean Tavern, 1986. Back (L to R): Jim Watson (trustee), Willie Yuill (manager), Roy Davidson (trustee), Vic Laing (trustee). Front: John McNeill (trustee), Jim Green (trust chairman), Geoff Craythorne (secretary and accountant).

The Dean Tavern, 1986. The former lounge bar upstairs is now a store. There are two lounge bars downstairs.

Tables set for the wedding reception of Mary Morrison and Brian Oliver (1962). This was the first reception in the new function suite.

Newtongrange guides and scouts on parade (1950s).

Lady Victoria Pipe Band (late 1950s).

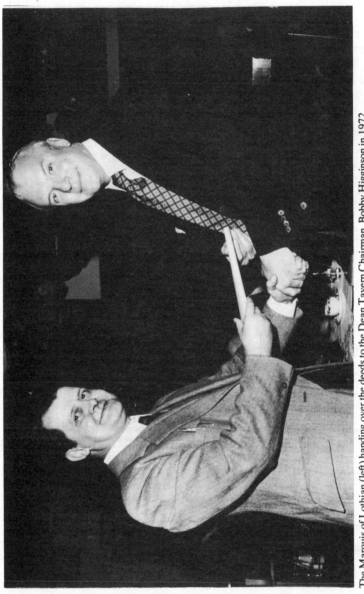

The Marquis of Lothian (left) handing over the deeds to the Dean Tavern Chairman, Bobby Higginson in 1972.

Glossary

Allan's Church - The Church of Christ.

bona fide traveller - someone who had travelled at least 2 or 3 miles and was entitled to buy a drink in a hotel on a Sunday.

Bottom Shop - The Abbey Inn.

brush the roads - remove part of the roof or pavement of a working to heighten the roadway.

Chinks - Arniston nickname for Newtongrange folk.

Chipper Avenue - Mansfield Avenue. That was where the chip van used to park.

C.I.S.W.O. - Coal Industry Welfare Organisation.

clipe - tell tales.

contractor - man who employed miners on behalf of the Lothian Coal Co.

Coronation Brig - railway bridge over Murderdean Road, now demolished.

crack - chat.

Dalkeith - bottled beer brewed by McLennan and Urquart of Dalkeith.

Dean barry - barrow used by the Dean to deliver orders.

Dean Cream - sherry bottled for the Dean.

Doo Ball - the annual dance of the pigeon homing society.

Dougall's - Newbattle District Council Office. Mr. Dougall was clerk to the council for a long time.

THE DEAN TAVERN

face – exposed seam of coal in a mine

flit - move house.

Frothblowers - name for a group of old men who used to meet in the Dean.

gaff - a travelling theatre.

Germans - Newtongrange nickname for Arniston folk.

Goth - a pub where all or part of the profits are used to benefit the community.

green table - Mungo MacKay had a green table in his office and if you were up before the green table you were probably in trouble.

guid brother - brother in law.

hogget - a hogshead

howk - dig

idle day - day off.

jug bar - a room in a pub where drink could be bought to drink off the premises. You took a jug for a pint of beer.

lowse – finish work

ane - this path with high brick walls ran across the middle of the park.

manhole - alcove in the Dean Tavern.

Nitten - Newtongrange.

Nitten Bull - Arniston nickname for Newtongrange folk.

Pay Friday - miners worked an eleven day fortnight and were paid every second Friday, Pay Friday.

Pay Saturday - the idle day after Pay Friday.

Penny a boot - a system worked in the pit where men work together as a team and were paid jointly.

pitch and toss - a gambling game where two coins are tossed in the air and bets laid on how they will land.

pot boy — a boy employed to do odd jobs in a public house

P.S.A. - Pleasant Sunday Afternoon Brotherhood, a Sunday afternoon musical concert for men.

redd - waste material from the pit, especially slag, from the boiler fires or stone from the picking tables.

residenter – a resident of very long standing

skin in - get in free, by stealth.

Square Heid - Newtongrange nickname for Arniston folk.

The Peth - the road between Newtongrange and Newbattle.

The Strip - the ground between the White Gates and the Bryans.

Tin Kirk - Ebeneezer Church.

Top Club - the Miner's Club, Newtongrange Community Association Social Club.

treckle - treacle.

Treckle Bekky - if you did not behave you were threatened that "Trekkle Bekky will get you!" She reputedly lived in a big pool at the Bryans.

up the braes - Arniston.

up the stairs - Mungo MacKay's office.

Vesting Day - January 1st. 1947, the day the pits were nationalised.

147

waiter - barman.

White Gates - the cross roads near the Dean Tavern where there used to be a level crossing on the pit railway line.

Appendix 2

Dean Tavern Committee Members
(from 1971 Dean Tavern Trustees)

John Callender	1899 - 1917	Lothian Coal Co.
Mungo MacKay	1899 - 1939	Lothian Coal Co.
James Hood	1899 - 1917	Lothian Coal Co.
James Taylor	1899 - 1915	
William Pryde	1899 - 1924	
David Pryde	1915 - 1922	
James Murray	1917 - 1945	Lothian Coal Co.
John Meek	1922 - 1936	
David Reid	1924 - 1932	
William Darge	1932 - 1952	
John Ross	1936 - 1953	
George MacKay	1939 - 1973	Lothian Coal Co.
David Haldane	1948 - 1965	
Andrew Aikman	1948 - 1965	manager, Dean Tavern
George Finlay	1952 - 1954	
John Rutherford	1954 - 1966	
Andrew Ross	1965 - 1969	
Tom Irvine	1970 - 1984	
Guy Stobbs	1971 - 1979	C.I.S.W.O.
*Bill Cook	1971 -	Newtongrange Community Association
Robert Higginson	1971 - 1975	Midlothian District Council
Harry McGowan	1971 - 1971	Bank of Scotland
Alan Landels	1971 - 1973	Bank of Scotland
George Gillespie	- 1984	C.I.S.W.O.
Robert Craik	1973 - 1983	Bank of Scotland
*John McNeill	1974 -	
William Steele	1975 - 1984	Midlothian District Council
Alex. Doolan	1979 -	C.I.S.W.O.

*Vic Laing	1984 -	C.I.S.W.O.
*Roy Davidson	1984 -	Bank of Scotland
*James Green	1984 -	Midlothian District Council
*James Watson	1984 -	

*Currently Trustees

Dean Tavern Office Bearers, etc.

Chairman

James Hood	1899 - 1917
Mungo MacKay	1917 - 1939
James Murray	1939 - 1945
George MacKay	1945 - 1950
Andrew Aikman	1950 - 1965
George MacKay	1965 - 1972
Robert Higginson	1972 - 1975
William Steel	1975 - 1984
James Green	1984 -

Secretaries

James Gilmour	1899 - 1951
A.C. Simpson	1951 - 1952
N.S. Currie	1952 - 1970
Geoffrey Craythorne	1970 -

Managers

Andrew Anderson	1899 - 1907
John Hood	1907 - 1915
John Purves	1916 - 1923
Thomas Hackett	1924 - 1934
Andrew Aikman	1934 - 1971
William Yuill	1971 -

Licence Holders

Andrew Anderson	1899 - 1907
John Gilmour	1907 - 1951
Andrew Aikman	1951 - 1971
William Yuill	1971 -

149

Appendix 3

Buildings Erected or Owned by the Dean Tavern

1902 Bowling green and pavilion	?
Newtongrange public park	?
Quoiting house, Easthouses	?
1906 Cricket pitch and pavilion	£316
1909 Rifle range	£89
1910 Dean Tavern	£3,081
1911 Newbattle Institute	£2,914
Band hall	£488
Easthouses football pavilion	?
1912 Pigeon house	?
1913 Institute extension	£2,543
1914 Picture house and shops	£6,440
1920 Nurse's cottage	£1,500
1923 Star Park and pavilion	£5,000
1925 Easthouses Institute	£4,000
1926 Two houses at picture house	?
1933 Garages for nurse and cinema manager	?
1939 The former United Free Church bought	£250
1943 Institute transferred to Welfare	-
1946 United Free Church sold to Masons	£600

1948 Star Park and pavilion transferred to Newtongrange Star   -

1949 Shops at picture house sold   £4,300
     Nurse's cottage transferred to Welfare   -

1954 Off Licence built at Dean Tavern   £1,400

1960 Dean Tavern extension built   £20,000

1962 Picture house sold to Midlothian County Council   £5,300

1972 Dean bought feus of Dean Tavern and bowling from Marquis of
     Lothian   £2,000

1976 Bowling green shed built   ?

1979 Bowling green and pavilion leased to Bowling Club   -

Appendix 4

Other Local Goths

The Black Bull Inn at Dalkeith was opened in 1905 by the Dalkeith Public House and Improvement Society. Shares were sold and profits were restricted to 5% (an excellent rate of return then). Any profit above that figure was to be spent on the welfare of the community. The company was wound up in the 1920s but the Black Bull is still 'the Goth' in Dalkeith.

In 1911, James Black, the licensee at Stobhill Inn was allowed to transfer the Stobhill licence to a new pub at Hunterfield, the Hunterfield Tavern. Both premises belonged to the Arniston Coal Co. which proposed to run the new pubs as a Gothenburg. Though it has long since been a brewery pub, Gorebridge people know it as 'the Goth'. The profits paid for the building of the Dundas Hall Picture House in the 1920s. It is not clear how the Hunterfield ceased to be a Goth and there appear to be no surviving records.

There was also a Goth at Niddrie probably begun by the Niddrie and Benhar Coal Co.

Appendix 5

List of Local Events

1795 Newbattle Paper Mill began

1802 Road between Eskbank and Newtonloan opened

1805 Newtonloan Toll began

1831 Innocent Railway began
Mineral railway to Lingerwood began
First viaduct at Lothian Bridge built

1835 First colliery houses at Newton Grange built
New parish school at Crawlees built

1837 Strike at Newbattle Collieries (3 months)

1838 New pit at East Bryans opened

1839 Lingerwood pit rebuilt

1840 Newbattle Brick and Tile Works opened
First pit ponies used underground

1842 Colliery School began at Galadalehill

1846 Millhill House built

1847 Main railway line to Edinburgh opened
Dalhousie Station opened
New Viaduct at Lothian Bridge built

1849 Newton Grange Colliery Schools built

1861 Lingerwood Pit shaft deepened to 888 feet

1870 Newton Grange House built

1871 Red Lion House built

1872 Six houses at St. Davids built

1873 Strike (7 weeks)
    Newbattle Gasworks opened

1874 Abbey Granary built
    Romans's Building built
    First Free Church built

1875 Good Templar Lodge 'Lothian Star' began
    Good Templar Hall built
    Newtonrange Flower Show and Industrial Society began

1879 Newtongrange Lothian Cricket Club began

1880 Second Free Church building
    Lothian Lodge of the Independent Order of Scottish Mechanics
began

1881 Cowden Grange built

1884 Newtongrange Colliery School extended

1886 Free Church Manse built

1890 Lothian Coal Company began
    Newbattle Paper Mill closed

1892 Lothian Cycling Club began

1893 Newbattle Public School opened
    Newtongrange Colliery School closed
    School at Crawlees closed
    Lothian Halls began
    Strike at Newbattle Collieries (9 weeks)

1894 Newbattle Paper Mill demolished
    Strike at Newbattle Collieries (17 weeks)
    Lothian Brass Band began

1895 Lady Victoria Pit opened
Newtongrange Star F.C. became a junior team

1896 Whitehill and Newbattle Building Company began
Newbattle and Dalkeith Golf Club began

1897 Abbey Inn began

1898 First houses built at Dean Park

1899 Dean Tavern built
First houses built at Monkswood

1902 Newtongrange Bowling Green opened
Newton House built
Newtongrange Ornithological Society began

1903 Newtongrange Star pavilion built

1904 Newtongrange Homing Society began

1906 Public park improved
New cricket pitch and pavilion opened
Reid's Buildings built
Arbuthnot Cottage built
Stewart's shop built

1907 Newbattle Public School extension built

1908 Newtongrange Station built
Dalhousie Station closed
Gorebridge Co-op Store built
Miniature Rifle Range built

1909 Saughs Cottages built
Masonic Lodge Newbattle St. Mary began
First nurse's cottage built
Newbattle Colliery Employees Nursing Association began

APPENDICES

1910 Easthouses Mine opened
Bryans Pit closed
Women's Liberal Association began
New Dean Tavern opened

1911 Y.W.C.A. began
Band Hall built
Newtongrange Institute opened

1912 Strike at Newbattle Collieries (6 weeks)
Monkswood re-named

1913 Newtongrange Gala Day began
Newtongrange Cage Bird Fanciers Association begun

1914 The Square built
Addition to Newtongrange Institute built
Newtongrange St Andrews Ambulance Association began
First public phone
Branch of Dalkeith Savings Bank opened

1915 Newtongrange Picture Palace
Ambulance Association began

1920 Newbattle Miners Welfare Committee began
Second nurse's cottage built

1921 Strike at Newbattle Collieries (3 months)

1922 Newtongrange Lawn Tennis Club began

1923 Last pit ponies underground

1924 Victoria Park and pavilion opened
Lothian Terrace built

1925 Easthouses Institute built
Newtongrange Primary School built

1926 Newtongrange Welfare Park opened
Strike at Newbattle Collieries (7 months)

1928 Newbattle Parish Council ended

1929 Free church building first used as Newtongrange Parish
Church

1932 Back kitchens and baths put in houses

1933 Gardiner's Place (first council scheme) built
Allan's Garage began
Old Abbeyland demolished
First talkies at the picture house

1936 Galadean built

1937 Newbattle and District Welfare Pipe Band began
Newbattle District Council Offices opened
Newbattle Abbey College began

1939 Newtongrange Parish Church hall built
Newtongrange Juvenile Pipe Band began

1940 Masterton House demolished

1942 Newtongrange Parish Church built

1945 Electric street lighting began

1946 Masonic Lodge bought old Free Church

1947 N.C.B. Vesting Day

1948 St Annes Roman Catholic Church began

1950 County Council took over Welfare Park
Welfare Pipe Band finished up
Brickworks closed

1953 Esk Valley College began at Lingerwood
Pithead Baths built at Easthouses
Newbattle Institute ended

1954 Pithead Baths built at Newtongrange

1956 Gasworks closed

1960 Easthouses pit closed
Picture house closed

1962 Mainline railway closed to passengers
Dean Tavern extension built
New Bowling Green Pavilion built

1965 Newtongrange Library opened

1967 Lingerwood Pit closed

1969 Mainline railway closed to freight
Newbattle High School opened
Easthouses Mine closed
Esk Valley College moved to Eskbank
Newbattle Swimming Pool opened

1971 Dean Trust formed

1972 Strike at Lady Victoria Pit (8 weeks)

1974 Strike at Lady Victoria Pit (4 weeks)

1976 Newtongrange Community Council began

1981 Lady Victoria Pit closed

1983 St. Anne's Sheltered Housing built

Appendix 6

P & D Lyle's Directory 1915

NEWTONGRANGE

POST OFFICE - Miss Letitia F. Armstrong, postmistress.
Postal Deliveries -7.35 a.m.; 4.15 p.m. Despatches Noon 6.30 p.m.

MASONIC LODGE, NEWBATTLE ST MARY, 1603 - R.W.M. Geo. Humphrey: S.W. William Carson; J.W. Andrew Brown; Secretary W Pryde; Treasurer, D Cossar.

NEWBATTLE BURNS CLUB - President, G. Humphrey; Vice-Pres., W. Carson Secretary, John Samuel.

NEWTONGRANGE CAGE BIRD SOCIETY - President, A. M. Gardiner; Vice-president, W. Thomson; Secretary and Treasurer - John Nelson.

LIBERAL ASSOCIATION - President, Alex Wilkie; Treasurer, Thos Liddle; Interim Secretary, A Wilkie

NEWBATTLE WOMEN'S UNIONIST ASSOCIATION - President Lady Anne Kerr, Vice-president, Mrs Hood and Mrs MacKay; Secretary, Mrs Gilmour.

NEWTONGRANGE MINIATURE RIFLE CLUB - Hon. President, J.A. Hood, Hon. Vice President, John Callender and Dr Easterbrook; President, W. Carson; Vice-president, J. Briggs; Treasurer, W.C. Kirkwood; Secretary A. Naysmith.

NEWTONGRANGE SILVER INSTRUMENTAL BAND - Conductor, James Brown.

NEWTONGRANGE WOMEN'S LIBERAL ASSOCIATION - President, Mrs Wilkie; Secretary Miss B. Cossar.

P.S.A. BROTHERHOOD - Hon. President, John Callender, Rev Wm Lindsay, Rev A. Hardie; President, Alex Wilkie; Vice Presidents, James Snodgrass, John I. Alison, G.F. Lamb, W. Fowler, A.M. Hardie, William Scott, J. Murray, J. Learmonth, W. Walker, A. Spark; Secy. David Pearson; Treas., Walter Young; Assistant Treasurer, J. Dick.

Armistead, Johnson N., bootmaker
Balmer, Thos., station agent
Bishop, Alex., gas manager, 131 Abbeyland
Callender, John, secy., Lothian Coal Co.
Campbell, John, cycle maker

Carson, Wm., underground manager
Clapperton, John, fruiterer
Dalkeith Co-operative Store branch
Danish Dairy Co
Dean tavern - John R. Hood, manager
Deans, Francis P., clerk, Saughs cotts
Dick, John Y., bootmaker
Erskine, David S., Black cot
Finlay, Wm., fruiterer
Fowler, Wm., Newbattle public school
Gardiner, Alex., hairdresser. Reid's bldgs.
Gorebridge Co-operative Store branch
Hackett, Thos., grocer
Hardie, Rev. Alex., U.F. Church manse
Humphrey, George, engineer, Saughs cotts
Inglis, Thos, 42 Deanpark
Kerr, M. & I., drapers
King. Robert. dairyman, 66 Abbey land
Ledingham, W., constable, 18 Deanpark
Knox, Geo, branch store manager
Liddle, David, overseer Saughs cotts
Lothian Coal Co., Ltd, Newbattle collieries
MacKay, Mungo, manager, Lingerwood
McDermott, John, hairdresser, Loan
McKenzie, Dr John, Old Schoolhouse
McNab, W.G., Newtongrange pharmacy
Mitchell, Miss, Old Schoolhouse
Moffat, James, water bailiff
Morris, John, grocer. Loan
Muir, Jas, grieve, Lingerwood farm house
Quinto, Burgari, restaurateur
Park, James, foreman, Saugh's cotts
Reid, Jas, and Wm., drapers
Reid, John, carrier, Gate house
Romans, Miss H.J., Newtongrange ho
Santini & Coy., restaurateurs
Scott, Richard, overseer, Saugh's cotts
Smith, Mrs E., merchant, Heath house
Spark, Alex., inspector of poor
Stark, Wm., N., janitor, Newbattle school

Stewart, Thomas, grocer, etc.
Trotter, Wm., tailor
Walker, Wm. L. publican
Watson, Wm., bootmaker
Watt, Wm., Newtongrange dairy
Whitcomb, Miss Agnes, Ury cottage

Appendix 7

The Silver Band

Adam Haldane: *"They've aye had a great band in Newtongrange, ye know – well, sometimes it was guid and sometimes it wisnae sae guid. But it was like everything else it had its ups and doons."*

The history of the present bank dates back to 1893 when the Newtongrange Lothian Brass Bank was founded. There had been an earlier band called the Marquis of Lothian's Band (and presumably funded by him) and the new band acquired some of the old bank's instruments and some from a Volunteer Band in Dalkeith. At first the members each contributed 6d a week to keep the band going but then a voluntary subscription of 1d a week from the men at the pit was started up and this raised £70 – £80 a year. The band also held weekly dances and organised the annual Newtongrange Games to help meet their expenses, which were considerable. A professional conductor was employed at a salary of £110 a year, uniforms and instruments had to be bought and maintained and travelling expenses to competitions had to be found. The village took a great pride in their band and it was important that it was well turned out.

The Lothian Coal Co. supported the band in a number of ways. Jobs and houses were made available for incoming players, shifts were changed to suit the band members and wages lost through playing engagements were made up by the company. Mr. Callender, the company secretary, took a keen interest in the bank and Mr. Mackay, the general manager, was band president for a number of years.

In 1909, a deputation from the band approached Mr. Callender to seek help. The band had nowhere regular to practice. They used the Lothian Halls when they could get a let, which was not often, or they rented a room at the Dean Tavern, which was not really suitable. The Dean Committee agreed to build a hall for the band and the Masonic Lodge. It was decided that the Dean should run the hall and all profits would go to the band but, in fact, the Lothian Coal

Co. took charge and lets had always to be arranged through the colliery office. The band hall was formally opened on Saturday 25th November 1911.

The band had bought a number of new instruments in 1901 with help from the Dean and the Lothian Coal Co. but a request was put into the Dean Committee in 1911 for new instruments "so they may be the better able to compete with others." The Dean footed the bill of £390 and the old instruments were kept for the junior band. The band was now a silver band and had been since 1905 when the old instruments had been silver-plated.

In 1914 the band competed at various contests at Hamilton, Falkirk, Motherwell, Prestonpans, Stoneyburn, Waverly Market, Murrayfield, Musselburgh and the Marine Gardens, Portobello as well as organising their own competition at Newtongrange. The band always fared quite well without winning very much in those days.

In 1926 the administration of the the silver band was taken over by Newbattle Miners Welfare Committee. Relations between the band and the Welfare Committee were by no means good and, when a request for new instruments was turned down by the committee in 1930, the band broke up citing "apathy of the general public and the bandsmen, absenteeism and disagreement with the management."

The band was re-started in 1932 and two years later the Welfare Committee did provide new instruments. In 1936, the Welfare requested that the band play once a week at Newtongrange and once a fortnight at Easthouses. The performances in the Welfare Park bandstand were great occasions and hundreds turned up to watch, listen and dance to the music. All band engagements in Newtongrange and Easthouses were free but the band took fees for performances elsewhere. Generally the cash from fees and any contest prize money was divided amongst the players but some of the money had to be returned to Welfare funds.

The band uniforms were in a bad state, as they were 24 years old, and in 1939 new uniforms were bought with money allocated by the Dean Committee. *"The equipment was of the very best. The Committee wished to see the Bandsmen fitted before payment was made and it was hoped the Band would appear in Public fully dressed."*

After the war there continued to be bad feeling between the silver band and the Welfare Committee, which refused to pay for a professional conductor, or for the band to compete in competitions. The silver band felt they were entitled to ½d from each miners' Welfare contribution but the local Welfare Committee was in debt and could pay no more. The band threatened to break away but the instruments belonged to the Welfare and they would have claimed them back. There was a suggestion in 1946 that the Lothian Coal Co. might take over the band.

The Dean and the Silver Band had always had a close relationship and the Dean had supported the band generously from the beginning. In the late 1940s, however, the Dean partially withdrew its support, contending that the Welfare should fulfill their responsibilities to the band. There was even an attempt by the Dean Committee to give the Band Hall to the Scouts in 1948 but the National Coal Board claimed ownership of the hall. The Dean Committee never resisted this claim as they were glad not to have the burden of maintenance.

The Welfare increased its support to the band in 1948 with a donation of £130, compared to £88 the year before and £46 in 1945. This enabled the band to take part in contests and the standard of playing improved under bandmaster James Farrow to the extent that the band took first prize in the third section at Kirkcaldy in 1952.

By 1953 with money "*more fluent in Welfare circles*" the Welfare Committee agreed to spend £90 for instrument repairs, £60 on uniforms and £200 to send the band to Manchester for the British Brass Band Championship Finals.

In 1954 'The Dean Tavern Committee Trophy' was presented by the Committee for a brass band competition at Dalkeith and the next year £100 was given to the band for uniforms. In recent years the Dean has given the Silver Band an annual grant, currently £350 a year. The band now lease the Band Hall from the Lothian Estates and have a club licence. They sometimes play in the Dean and that is always a special occasion. In October 1986, the band played in the Dean the night before they left on a visit to Hungary and there's always a performance on New Year's Day.

The band has done well in competitions recently. In 1980 they won the British Championship (Second Section) and they have appeared on T.V. Formerly the Silver Band was supported by contributions from the Lady Vic and then from Bilston Glen Pit but in 1985 the union withdrew its support after a dispute with the band. Since then, the band has found commercial sponsorship and is now called Scottish Brewers Silver Band (Newtongrange).

Appendix 8

The Pipe Bands

The first adult pipe band in Newtongrange was the Newbattle and District Welfare Pipe Band* founded in 1937 under Pipe Major Scott. Some of the men at the pit paid ½d a week for the band and the Dean Committee gave a loan of £94 for pipes and drums. This was repaid by 1944. The band folded in 1950 and the Welfare Committee tried to reclaim the uniforms and instruments but only one uniform was ever handed back.

Another pipe band was started up in 1939. Two boys, John Grant and James Peacock went round all the doors in Newtongrange asking for names of boys who wanted to join a pipe band. Forty names were collected and the Newtongrange Juvenile Pipe Band was formed. Pipe Major Sandy McIntosh tutored them and the Dean gave them £150 to buy uniforms – they wore the shepherd tartan with blue jerkins. Between 1940 and 1948 the boy's pipe band raised £17,000 for charity and in 1944 won every contest they entered. Three years in a row, 1948, 1949 and 1950, the band won the World Juvenile Pipe Band Championship. At 18, some of the boys were too old to play in juvenile competitions so an adult band, Newtongrange Lothian Pipe Band, was begun but it was just the same lads (bar two) under a different name. In 1950 the bands were 1st in the Juvenile, 1st in Grade 3, 1st in Grade 2 and 4th in the Open category, at the Miner's Gala in Edinburgh. A number of girls joined the band and later a Girl's Pipe Band was formed.

The Dean Committee gave the Boy's pipe band a loan of £300 to buy new kilts in 1950. The money was not repaid by 1956 and rumours reached the Committee that the pipe band were selling the uniforms.

The band took an new name in 1954, Lady Victoria Pipe Band, when an arrangement was made for 1d a week to be collected from some of the men at the pit. It was no longer a juvenile band. Since the Lady Vic closed in 1981 the pipe band has had a connection with Bilston Glen Pit, where the men contribute 3p a week. The band is now called Newtongrange and Bilston Colliery Pipe Band and is still going strong under Pipe Major Tom Wilson

His predecessor, Bill Peacock, remembers playing in one competiton in which eight good pipers were needed. The Lothian Pipe Band had only seven players good enough to take part in the competition. The eighth player was OK on the chanter but forgot all the tunes as soon as he had the pipes under his

*There was a Boy's Brigade Pipe Band in the 1920s

oxter. They put him in with dummy reeds so he couldn't be heard. The judges never knew there was a dummy piper as they were under cover.

The pipe band used to play round the park after the gala and then march single file into the Dean and play round the bar.

Appendix 9

Easthouses

Easthouses had been a colliery village for hundreds of years before the village of Newtongrange was built. The Easthouses men were great exponents of quoiting (pronounced 'kiting') and cock fighting.

The Marquis of Lothian's Colliery School was at Easthouses until 1849 when he built one at Newtongrange and there was still an infant school in the village until well into this century. Easthouses Drift mine was opened in 1910 and closed in 1960. Throughout the nineteenth century the population of the village fluctuated between three and four hundred and it was not until 1924, when Bogwood housing scheme was begun by the Lothian Coal Co., that the village expanded much.

Easthouses has always retained its own identity despite the nearness of Newtongrange on one side and the sprawling modern housing scheme of Mayfield adjacent to the south. Previously Easthouses had a Burns Club, a homing society, its own gala day and a flower show. Easthouses Lily was their junior football team and the Dean built them a pavilion in 1911. In 1929 the football pitch was taken over to make a Welfare Park land a new pitch was built at the other side of the village, but it now lies unused and derelict.

The Easthouses professional games were famous before the First World War and these were revived for a few years as amateur games in the 1930s. An Institute was built with Dean Tavern money in 1925 and the building is now a Miners' Welfare Club with a licence. In 1934 a bowling green and pavilion was built in the park. A public house, the Barley Bree, opened in 1949.

Appendix 10

Rosewell

The Lothian Coal Co. owned two pits outside Newtongrange, Polton Pit at Bonnyrigg and Whitehill Pit at Rosewell. Polton Pit was small and, though the Coal Co. built a number of miner's houses in Bonnyrigg. it had no influence in the running of the burgh. Rosewell was different, the village being wholly owned by the Coal Company. Mr. Hood had first leased Whitehill Pit from Mr. Wardlaw Ramsay of Whitehill in 1856. Four years later, on the initiative of Mr. Hood, Rosewell Co-op was founded, the first in Midlothian.

Rosewell got its bowling green in 1901 at the expense of the Lothian Coal Co. and with some money from the Rosewell Co-op, Rosewell Tavern, the first public house in the village, opened in 1909 and was run by the Co-op. It was never a Gothenburg but the Coal Co. stipulated that a certain proportion of the profits should be spent for the benefit of the community.

Until the 1890s, Rosewell was bigger than Newtongrange but, from 1898, Newtongrange far outstripped Rosewell in size. Although Mungo Mackay was general manager for all five pits, the day-to-day authority in Roswell lay with the Whitehill manager, Mr. Hamilton. Like Mr. Mackay, he exercised great control over 'his' village and he was feared by the villagers.

Population

	Newtongrange	Easthouses
1911	4,090	390
1921	4,817*	
1931	6,171*	
1933	7,000	
1950	7,500	

*including Easthouses

Number of Men Employed at Newbattle Colliery

1834 –	279	1945 –	2800
1840 –	400	1947 –	2083
1842 –	360	1948 –	2274
1856 –	500	1949 –	2529
1875 –	500	1950 –	2695
1893 –	900	1954 –	4000
1902 –	1200	1973 –	909
1916 –	2000	1974 –	900
1935 –	3000	1981 –	570

Published Sources

Mining in Mid and East Lothian: A.S. Cunningham, 1925.

Licensing and Temperance in Sweden, Norway and Denmark: E.A. Pratt, 1907.

Ale an' A' thing: Veronica Hartwich, 1980.

Village Story: Ken Laird.

Political and Social Movements in Dalkeith: Alexander Mitchell.

Prestonpans, Scotland's Last Saltworks: Alexander Hamilton.

Industries of Scotland: David Bremner, 1869

A History of the Scottish People 1560-1830: T.C. Smout, 1969.

Around Dalkeith and Camp Meg: J. C. Carrick, 1912.

Early Mining in Arniston and Newbattle: Sandy Fairlie.

A History of the Brewing Industry in Scotland: Ian Donnachie, 1979.

A History of the Scottish Miners: R. Page Arnot, 1955.

My Life with the Miners: Abe Moffat, 1965.

A Short History of Scotland: R.L. Mackie, 1961.

Right of Way: John Romans, 1870.

Neubottil Newbattle: Newbattle High School.

Odyssey: Ian MacDougall, 1982.

The Franks Parliamentary Commission, 1840.

Scottish Mining Museum Research Papers: Michael Cotterill and Colin Denovan.

1st Statistical Account of Scotland.

2nd Statistical Account of Scotland.

3rd Statistical Account of Scotland.

Dalkeith Advertiser, 1869-1986.

The Scotsman, 23 March 1880.

The Concise Scots Dictionary, 1985.

Edinburgh Post Office Directories.

Unpublished Sources

Dean Committee Minutes 1899-1986.

Midlothian Licensing Court Records 1829-1986.,

Register of Sasines.

Silver Band Minute Book.

Appendix 13

Acknowledgements

I am grateful to the following people for the help they have given to me in my research into the history of Newtongrange:
Bill Peacock, Adam Haldane, Jim Reid, Stevie Moore, Bob Herriot, Davie Moffat, Andrew Samuel, Abie Walker, Alex. Trench, Tom Wilson, Jim Barton, Mrs. Barton, Dave O'Connor, Mrs. Preston, Tom Reid, Drew Aitken, George Armstrong, Mrs. Armstrong, Katherine McKerrow, Jim Green, Anne Green, Jim Watson, Mrs. Henderson, Scott Ballantyne, James Smith, Neil Allan, Charlie McMaster, Vic Laing, Mike Cotterill, Colin Denovan, Geoff Craythorne, Willie Yuill, Cathy Yuill, Rob Ross, Ella Sked, Kevin Brown, Peter Tajasque, Margaret McLean, Brian Osborne, the late Tommy Thomson, Joe Gardiner, Mr. And Mrs. Kim Reid, John Lockhart, Mrs. and Mrs. Tony Campbell, Tom Lockhart, George Pitcher, Pat Murray, Norrie Jamieson, Frances Bell, Sheena Johnstone, Sybil Kinghorn, the late Dod Hay, Kerr and Annabel McGregor, Mr. Cummings, Anderson Duncan, Andrew Anderson, John Jenks.